# 중학 영어의
# 결정적 단어들

동사

＊ 본 도서는 2017년 출간된 〈중학교 가기 전에 끝내는 영단어〉의 동일한 내용 개정판입니다.

**중학 영어의
결정적 단어들** 동사

**지은이** AST Jr. English Lab
**감수** Steve Brown, 조희
**초판 1쇄 발행** 2017년 12월 10일
**개정판 1쇄 인쇄** 2024년 11월 21일
**개정판 1쇄 출간** 2024년 11월 29일

**발행인** 박효상 **편집장** 김현 **기획 · 편집** 장경희, 이한경 **디자인** 임정현
**표지디자인** 문예진 **마케팅** 이태호, 이전희 **관리** 김태옥
**종이** 월드페이퍼 **인쇄 · 제본** 예림인쇄 · 바인딩

**출판등록** 제10-1835호 **발행처** 사람in
**주소** 121-839 서울시 마포구 양화로 11길 14-10 (서교동) 3F
**전화** 02) 338-3555(代) **팩스** 02) 338-3545
**E-mail** saramin@netsgo.com **Website** www.saramin.com

ISBN
979-11-7101-017-2 64740
979-11-7101-014-1 (세트)

우아한 지적만보, 기민한 실사구시 **사람in**

# 중학 영어의
# 결정적 단어들

동
사

AST Jr. English Lab 지음

사람in
saram
in.com

# 목차

# 이렇게 활용하세요!

초등 교과서가 그림과 활동들로 흥미롭게 구성되어 있는 반면, 중학 교과서에는 낯선 영어 단어들과 표현들이 가득해요. 초등 영어가 재미로 가득했다면 중등 영어에서는 '공부'로써의 영어와 만나게 되는 거예요. 그렇기 때문에 예비 중학생들이 가장 먼저 해야 할 일은 영어 어휘력 쌓기예요. 보통 학생들이 일찍 영어를 배웠지만 의외로 단어를 정확히 알지 못해요. 그동안 상황과 느낌으로 대강 단어를 찍었다면 이제 단어의 정확한 뜻과 사용법을 익혀야 해요.

단어 중에서도 동사는 문장의 구조를 세우고 전체 문장을 지배하기 때문에 가장 중요해요. 주어와 동사만 알맞게 갖추어도 영어 문장을 뚝딱 만들 수 있죠. 이것은 학교 영어뿐만 아니라 읽기, 듣기, 말하기, 쓰기 모두에 해당하니 지금부터 탄탄하게 기초 동사를 다지는 것이 좋겠죠? 이 책으로 차근차근 시작할 수 있도록 교육부에서 제시한 중학 필수 기본 어휘 중 동사만 엄선하여 체계적으로 구성했어요. 이 책을 마칠 때쯤 동사와 더불어 문장 구조까지 잡을 수 있을 거예요.

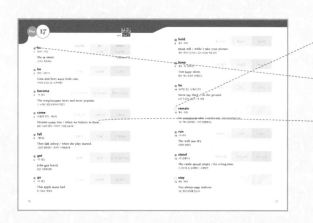

■의 동사는 규칙적으로 변해요. 빈칸에 알맞게 써 넣어 보세요.
■의 동사는 불규칙적으로 변해요. 제시된 단어를 따라 써 보세요.
● / 는 뒤의 단어들이 없어도 완벽한 문장이라는 표시예요. 문장 구조를 익히며 따라 읽어 보세요.

문제를 풀며 앞에서 배운 어휘들을 확실히 마무리하세요. 정답은 〈**www.saramin.com** → 자료실〉에서 다운로드 받을 수 있어요.

# 영어, 동사가 없으면 문장도 없다.

영어 단어는 동사, 명사, 형용사, 부사, 전치사, 접속사, 감탄사로 분류할 수 있어요.
그중 동사는 문장을 만들 때 꼭 필요한 뼈대예요.

I the guitar. (I 나, the guitar 기타) – 문장 ✕

이것만으로는 무슨 일이 일어나고 있는지 알 수가 없어요. 여기에 동사 play를 더해 봅시다.

I **play** the guitar. (play 연주하다) – 문장 ○

play 덕분에 I가 무엇 하는지를 알 수 있게 되었어요. 이처럼 동사는 동작을 나타내는 말로
'~하다', '~이다'라는 뜻이에요. 서술, 질문, 명령, 동작, 상태를 표현할 수 있어요.


I **play** the guitar. 나는 기타를 연주한다. _ 서술

Do you **like** this song? 너는 이 노래를 좋아하니? _ 질문

**Play** the music! 음악을 연주해라! _ 명령

I **played** soccer after school. 나는 방과 후에 **축구를 했다**. _ 동작

I **am** tired of studying. 나는 공부하기에 지쳤다. _ 상태


**연습문제** 다음 문장에서 동사를 찾아 동그라미 하세요.

1   Anna writes the letter.

2   We come from Switzerland.

3   I get up early every day.

4   Carol brushes her teeth twice a day.

5   I take the bus to school.

6   It rains a lot in summer.

7   They speak English at school.

8   He speaks German.

# 왜 영어 교과서 단어가 사전에 없을까?

- **rise** 뜨다

**The sun rises in the East.** 태양은 동쪽에서 뜬다.

**The sun rose this morning.** 오늘 아침 태양이 떴다.

어떤 일이 지금 일어날 수도, 미래에 일어날 수도, 과거에 일어났을 수도 있어요. 문장에서 이런 때의 차이를 보여주는 게 바로 동사예요. 동사는 때와 주어에 따라 모양이 바뀌어요.

**The sun rises in the East.** 태양은 동쪽에서 뜬다. (현재, 3인칭 단수 주어)

**The sun rose this morning.** 오늘 아침 태양이 떴다. (과거)

## 〈동사의 현재형〉

지금 일어나는 일을 말할 때 주어가 3인칭 단수(he, she, it …)이면 동사의 모양이 달라져요.

▶ 보통 끝에 s를 붙임.
　speak –speak**s**

▶ 동사가 –ss, –x, –ch, –sh,–o로 끝날 때 –es를 붙임.
　kiss – kiss**es**
　fix – fix**es**
　watch – watch**es**
　crush – crush**es**
　go – go**es**

▶ 동사가 「자음 + y」로 끝날 때 –y를 지우고 –ies를 붙임.
　carry – carr**ies**
　study – stud**ies**

연습문제 다음 문장을 알맞은 현재형 동사로 바꿔 쓰세요.

1  He go to school by bus.

2  She read a book.

3  Ms. Kim teach English.

4  The plane leave for Paris at 9:00.

## 〈동사의 과거형과 과거분사형〉

이미 일어난 일을 말할 때 동사는 모양이 바뀌어요.

▶ -e로 끝나는 동사는 끝에 -d를 붙임.

agree – agreed – agreed
love – loved – loved

▶ 「단모음 + 단자음」으로 끝나는 동사는 마지막 글자를 한 번 더 쓰고 -ed를 붙임.

stop – stopped – stopped

(예외) 2음절 이상의 단어는 마지막 음절에 강세가 있는 경우에만 해당

vísit – visited – visited

▶ 「자음 + y」로 끝나는 동사는 -y를 -ied로 고침.

carry – carried – carried
study – studied – studied

(예외) 「모음 + y」는 뒤에 -ed만 붙임.

play – played – played

▶ 불규칙적으로 변하는 경우도 있음.

cut – cut – cut
feel – felt – felt
begin – began – begun
come – came – come

**연습문제** 다음 문장을 과거형으로 바꾸세요.

1   He works hard.

2   She closes the door.

3   They cook dinner.

4   My mom comes home at 7.

5   We hug each other.

Pattern 1

## 주어 + 동사

| 주어 | 동사 | |
|------|------|---|
| These dogs<br>이 개들은 | bark<br>짖는다 | in the early morning.<br>이른 아침에 |
| The doctor<br>그 의사는 | looked at every patients.<br>모든 환자들을 진찰했다. | |

bark와 같은 완전자동사는 '주어'만 있으면 문장을 만들 수 있어요. 주로 동작이나 움직임을 표현하는 동사들이 이런 특징을 보여요. 그럼 in the early morning은 뭐냐고요? '이른 아침' 이라는 시간을 알려주는 부사구예요. 이를테면, 문장의 의미를 더욱 이해하기 쉽게 해주는 추가 설명이죠. 부사구는 문장 전체를 꾸며 시간, 장소, 방법 등을 알려줍니다.

두 번째 문장을 보면 자동사 look이 전치사 at과 함께 쓰여 '~을 자세히 보다; 진찰하다'라는 뜻의 구동사가 되었어요. 이런 구동사의 경우 전치사와 항상 함께 하기 때문에 동사 뒤에 / 표시를 생략했어요.

MP3

| | 3인칭/현재 | 과거 | 과거분사 |
|---|---|---|---|

☐ **act**
1 행동을 취하다, ~하게 굴다

Sue **acted** / nervously.
수는 행동했다 / 신경질적으로

☐ **bark**
2 짖다

A dog **barked** / as we passed.
개가 짖었다 / 우리가 지나갈 때

■ **bend**
3 구부리다

bends     bent     bent

The branch **bent** / in the wind.
나뭇가지가 휘었다 / 바람에

☐ **blink**
4 깜박거리다

The street light **blinked**.
가로등이 깜박거렸다.

☐ **cough**
5 기침을 하다

My brother **coughed**.
동생이 기침을 했다.

☐ **cry**
6 울다

Jean **cried** / all of a sudden.
진은 울었다 / 갑자기

☐ **dance**
7 춤추다

She **danced** / on the smooth floor.
그녀는 춤췄다 / 매끄러운 바닥에서

## dig
**8** (땅을) 파다

digs | dug | dug

They **dug** / deep for gold.
그들은 팠다 / 금을 찾으려고 깊게

## fall
**9** 떨어지다, 넘어지다

falls | fell | fallen

I **fell** over.
나는 넘어졌다.

## hold
**10** (계속) 잡고 있다, 지탱하다, 버티다

holds | held | held

**Hold** / still while I take your picture.
버텨 / 계속 내가 네 사진을 찍을 동안

## laugh
**11** 웃다

Don't **laugh at** me!
나를 비웃지 마!

## press
**12** 누르다, 밀다

Guilt **pressed** / upon him.
죄가 눌렀다 / 그를

## tell
**13** (비밀을) 말하다

tells | told | told

He won't **tell**.
그는 말하지 않을 것이다.

## sing
**14** 노래하다

sings | sang | sung

She **sings** / very well.
그녀는 노래한다 / 매우 잘

## stand
**15** 서다

stands | stood | stood

A herd of elephants **stood** / in the water.
코끼리 떼가 서있다 / 물에

## Mini Test

**A** 빈칸에 알맞은 단어를 〈보기〉에서 찾아 쓰세요.

**1** Sue _____ nervously.

수는 신경질적으로 행동했다.

**2** A dog _____ as we passed.

우리가 지나갈 때 개가 짖었다.

**3** The branch _____ in the wind.

나뭇가지가 바람에 휘었다.

**4** The street light _____.

가로등이 깜박였다.

**5** My brother _____.

동생이 기침을 했다.

**6** Jean _____ all of a sudden.

진은 갑자기 울었다.

**7** She _____ on the smooth floor.

그녀는 매끄러운 바닥에서 춤췄다.

**8** They _____ deep for gold.

그들은 금을 찾으려고 깊게 팠다.

**보기**

acted
bent
barked
blinked
cried
coughed
danced
dug

**B** 단어를 알맞게 배열하여 문장을 완성하세요.

**1**  fell    I    over.

**2**  while I    take your picture.    Hold still

**3**  laugh at    Don't    me!

**4**  Guilt    upon him.    pressed

**5**  tell.    He    won't

**6**  sings    She    very well.

**7**  stood    A herd of elephants    in the water.

12

C 다음 문장에서 동사를 찾아 동그라미하고, 해석을 써 보세요.

1 The street light blinked.

_____

2 She danced on the smooth floor.

_____

3 The branch bent in the wind.

_____

4 Sue acted nervously.

_____

5 My brother coughed.

_____

6 I fell over.

_____

7 A dog barked as we passed.

_____

8 They dug deep for gold.

_____

9 Jean cried all of a sudden.

_____

10 Don't laugh at me!

_____

11 Hold still while I take your picture.

_____

12 She sings very well.

_____

13 He won't tell.

_____

14 A herd of elephants stood in the water.

_____

15 Guilt pressed upon him.

_____

# Day 2

MP3

| | 3인칭/현재 | 과거 | 과거분사 |
|---|---|---|---|

**1 appear**
나타나다; ~처럼 보이다

A school bus **appeared** / over the bridge.
학교 버스가 나타났다 / 다리 위로

**2 arrive**
도착하다

Visitors will **arrive** / at 10 o'clock.
방문객들은 도착할 것이다 / 10시에

**3 begin** — begins / began / begun
시작하다, 시작되다

Jenny's journey **began** / in March.
제니의 여행은 시작되었다 / 3월에

**4 bow**
인사하다

Ed **bowed** / very gracefully.
에드는 인사했다 / 매우 기품 있게

**5 change**
변화하다

The weather **changed**.
날씨가 변했다.

**6 climb**
오르다

He **climbed** / over the fence.
그는 올라갔다 / 울타리 위로

**7 come** — comes / came / come
오다

Winter **came** / late this year.
겨울은 왔다 / 늦게 올해

14

☐ **disappear**

8  사라지다

Tropical forests **disappeared** / too quickly.
열대 우림은 사라졌다 / 너무 빠르게

☐ **exist**

9  존재하다

Dinosaurs no longer **exist**.
공룡은 더 이상 존재하지 않는다.

☐ **fill**

10  가득 차다

Her eyes **filled** / with water.
그녀의 눈은 가득 찼다 / 눈물로

☐ **finish**

11  끝나다

My plans never **finish**.
내 계획들은 결코 끝나지 않는다.

☐ **glance**

12  힐끗 보다

I **glanced** / at the clock.
나는 힐끗 봤다 / 시계를

■ **go**

13  가다

| goes | went | gone |
| --- | --- | --- |

I **go** / to school by bike.
나는 간다 / 학교에 자전거로

☐ **occur**

14  발생하다

The accident **occurred** / at 8:10 a.m.
그 사고는 발생했다 / 오전 8시 10분에

☐ **stop**

15  멈추다, 서다

The bus **stops** / at all stations.
그 버스는 선다 / 모든 정류장에

15

# Mini Test

**A** 빈칸에 알맞은 단어를 〈보기〉에서 찾아 쓰세요.

**1** A school bus _____ over the bridge.
학교 버스가 다리 위로 나타났다.

**2** Visitors will _____ at 10 o'clock.
방문객들은 열 시에 도착할 거다.

**3** Jenny's journey _____ in March.
제니의 여행은 3월에 시작되었다.

**4** Ed _____ very gracefully.
에드는 매우 기품 있게 인사했다.

**5** The weather _____.
날씨가 바뀌었다.

**6** He _____ over the fence.
그는 울타리 위로 올라갔다.

**7** Winter _____ late this year.
올해는 겨울이 늦게 왔다.

**8** Tropical forests _____ too quickly.
열대 우림은 너무 빠르게 사라졌다.

보기
came
changed
climbed
bowed
arrive
appeared
began
disappeared

**B** 단어를 알맞게 배열하여 문장을 완성하세요.

**1** no longer | exist. | Dinosaurs

**2** filled with | Her eyes | water.

**3** finish. | My plans | never

**4** glanced | I | at the clock.

**5** to school | I go | by bike.

**6** occurred | The accident | at 8:10 a.m.

**7** The bus | at all stations. | stops

C 다음 문장에서 동사를 찾아 동그라미하고, 해석을 써 보세요.

**1** He climbed over the fence.

_____

**2** I glanced at the clock.

_____

**3** I go to school by bike.

_____

**4** The bus stops at all stations.

_____

**5** Her eyes filled with water.

_____

**6** The accident occurred at 8:10 a.m.

_____

**7** My plans never finish.

_____

**8** Tropical forests disappeared too quickly.

_____

**9** A school bus appeared over the bridge.

_____

**10** Ed bowed very gracefully.

_____

**11** Winter came late this year.

_____

**12** Jenny's journey began in March.

_____

**13** The weather changed.

_____

**14** Dinosaurs no longer exist.

_____

**15** Visitors will arrive at 10 o'clock.

_____

MP3

| | 3인칭/현재 | 과거 | 과거분사 |
|---|---|---|---|

☐ **bake**

1  구워지다, 빵을 굽다

**Bake** / for 30 minutes.
구워라 / 30분 동안

◼ **burn**

2  (불이) 타오르다, 불에 타다

burns  burned/burnt  burned/burnt

The fire **burnt** / for a long time.
불은 타올랐다 / 오랫동안

◼ **burst**

3  터지다

bursts  burst  burst

The balloon **burst** / loudly.
그 풍선은 터졌다 / 큰소리로

☐ **cook**

4  요리하다

My dad **cooks** / for us.
우리 아빠는 요리한다 / 우리를 위해

◼ **eat**

5  먹다

eats  ate  eaten

Will you **eat** / at home tonight?
너는 먹을 거니 / 오늘밤 집에서?

◼ **fit**

6  맞다, 알맞다

fits  fitted/fit  fitted/fit

The jeans **fit** / perfectly.
그 청바지는 맞는다 / 완벽하게

☐ **float**

7  뜨다, 떠오르다

The paper boat **floated** / on the lake.
종이배가 떴다 / 호수 위에

**fry**

8 튀겨지다, 프라이가 되다

The onion **fried** / until golden brown.
양파는 튀겨졌다 / 황금 갈색이 될 때까지

**leak**

9 (액체 · 기체가) 새다

The roof of our class **leaks**.
우리 교실의 지붕이 샌다.

**open**

10 열리다

The door **opened**.
문이 열렸다.

**pack**

11 짐을 싸다, 포장이 되다

Jina simply **packed up**.
지나는 간단하게 짐을 쌌다.

**peel**

12 벗겨 떨어지다

The outer skin **peels** / off regularly.
바깥 껍질이 벗겨졌다 / 일정하게

**pile**

13 모이다, 쌓이다

Fallen leaves **piled up**.
낙엽이 쌓였다.

**prepare**

14 준비하다, 대비하다

We have to **prepare** / for the typhoon.
우리는 대비해야 한다 / 태풍에

**take care of**

15 ~를 보살피다

takes care of    took care of    taken care of

I **took care of** the dog.
나는 그 개를 돌봤다.

**A** 빈칸에 알맞은 단어를 〈보기〉에서 찾아 쓰세요.

**1** _____ for 30 minutes.

30분 동안 구워라.

**2** The fire _____ for a long time.

불은 오랫동안 타올랐다.

**3** The balloon _____ loudly.

그 풍선은 매우 크게 터졌다.

**4** My dad _____ for us.

아빠는 우리를 위해 요리한다.

**5** Will you _____ at home tonight?

너는 오늘밤 집에서 먹을 거니?

**6** The jeans _____ perfectly.

그 청바지는 완벽하게 맞는다.

**7** The paper boat _____ on the lake.

그 종이배는 호수에 떴다.

**8** The onion _____ until golden brown.

양파는 황금 갈색이 될 때까지 튀겨졌다.

> 보기
>
> floated
> burst
> burnt
> Bake
> cooks
> eat
> fit
> fried

**B** 단어를 알맞게 배열하여 문장을 완성하세요.

**1** of our class　　leaks.　　The roof

**2** opened.　　The door

**3** simply　　packed up.　　Jina

**4** peels　　off regularly.　　The outer skin

**5** Fallen leaves　　up.　　piled

**6** We have to　　for the typhoon.　　prepare

**7** I　　the dog.　　took care of

C 다음 문장에서 동사를 찾아 동그라미하고, 해석을 써 보세요.

**1** The fire burnt for a long time.

_____

**2** Fallen leaves piled up.

_____

**3** The balloon burst loudly.

_____

**4** I took care of the dog.

_____

**5** Will you eat at home tonight?

_____

**6** The jeans fit perfectly.

_____

**7** The paper boat floated on the lake.

_____

**8** The door opened.

_____

**9** The roof of our class leaks.

_____

**10** The onion fried until golden brown.

_____

**11** Jina simply packed up.

_____

**12** The outer skin peels off regularly.

_____

**13** My dad cooks for us.

_____

**14** We have to prepare for the typhoon.

_____

**15** Bake for 30 minutes.

_____

MP3

| | 3인칭/현재 | 과거 | 과거분사 |
|---|---|---|---|

**blow**
1 (입으로) 불다, (바람이) 불다

blows  blew  blown

A warm wind **blew** / from the south.
따뜻한 바람이 불었다 / 남쪽에서부터

**blossom**
2 꽃이 피다

All the trees **blossomed** / at the same time.
모든 나무가 꽃을 피웠다 / 동시에

**cooperate**
3 협력하다

He **cooperated** / with the police investigation.
그는 협조했다 / 경찰 조사관에게

**die**
4 죽다

Einstein **died** / when he was 76.
아인슈타인은 죽었다 / 76세에

**diminish**
5 줄어들다, 감소하다

Winds will slowly **diminish** / overnight.
바람은 천천히 줄어들 것이다 / 밤사이에

**escape**
6 탈출하다, 벗어나다

Captain Jean **escaped** / from the sinking ship.
진 선장은 탈출했다 / 침몰하는 배에서

**exercise**
7 운동을 하다

I **exercise** / regularly.
나는 운동한다 / 규칙적으로

## gather
**8** 모이다

Wild animals **gathered** / close to the town.
야생 동물들이 모였다 / 마을 가까이

## glow
**9** 타다, 빛나다

Some stones **glow** / in the dark.
어떤 돌들은 빛난다 / 어둠 속에서

## hunt
**10** 사냥하다, 추적하다, 뒤지다

Police **hunted** / for a missing child.
경찰은 추적했다 / 실종된 아이를

## invest
**11** 투자하다

We **invested** / in stocks.
우리는 투자했다 / 주식에

## jog
**12** 조깅하다

I **jog** / every morning.
나는 조깅한다 / 매일 아침에

## leave
**13** 떠나다

leaves     left     left

My mom **left** / for work at 6 a.m.
우리 엄마는 떠났다 / 아침 6시에 일하러

## lie
**14** 거짓말하다

She's **lying** / to you.
그녀는 거짓말하고 있다 / 너에게

## meet
**15** (우연히) 만나다

meets     met     met

When will we **meet** / again?
언제 우리가 만날까 / 다시?

**A** 빈칸에 알맞은 단어를 〈보기〉에서 찾아 쓰세요.

**1** A warm wind _____ from the south.
따뜻한 바람이 남쪽에서 불었다.

**2** All the trees _____ at the same time.
모든 나무들이 동시에 꽃을 피웠다.

**3** He _____ with the police investigation.
그는 경찰 조사관에게 협조했다.

**4** Einstein _____ when he was 76.
아이슈타인은 76세에 죽었다.

**5** Winds will slowly _____ overnight.
바람은 밤사이 천천히 줄어들 것이다.

**6** Captain Jean _____ from the sinking ship.
진 선장은 침몰하는 배에서 탈출했다.

**7** I _____ regularly.
나는 규칙적으로 운동한다.

**8** Wild animals _____ close to the town.
야생동물들이 마을 가까이 모였다.

보기
blossomed
blew
died
diminish
cooperated
escaped
gathered
exercise

**B** 단어를 알맞게 배열하여 문장을 완성하세요.

**1** Some stones | in the dark. | glow
_____

**2** hunted | Police | for a missing child.
_____

**3** invested | We | in stocks.
_____

**4** jog | I | every morning.
_____

**5** left | My mom | for work at 6 a.m.
_____

**6** lying | She's | to you.
_____

**7** again? | When will we | meet
_____

C  다음 문장에서 동사를 찾아 동그라미하고, 해석을 써 보세요.

1  Some stones glow in the dark.
_____

2  My mom left for work at 6 a.m.
_____

3  He cooperated with the police investigation.
_____

4  We invested in stocks.
_____

5  Winds will slowly diminish overnight.
_____

6  Captain Jean escaped from the sinking ship.
_____

7  I jog every morning.
_____

8  Wild animals gathered close to the town.
_____

9  All the trees blossomed at the same time.
_____

10  Police hunted for a missing child.
_____

11  A warm wind blew from the south.
_____

12  I exercise regularly.
_____

13  When will we meet again?
_____

14  She's lying to you.
_____

15  Einstein died when he was 76.
_____

# Day 5

MP3

| | 3인칭/현재 | 과거 | 과거분사 |
|---|---|---|---|

**☐ argue**

1 다투다

We **argued** / when we were little.
우리는 다퉜다 / 우리가 어렸을 때

**☐ balance**

2 균형을 잡다

She can **balance** / on one foot.
그녀는 균형을 잡을 수 있다 / 한 발로

**☐ behave**

3 행동하다

She didn't **behave** / badly.
그녀는 행동하지 않았다 / 나쁘게

**☐ bounce**

4 튀다, 튀어 오르다

The ball **bounced** / twice.
공이 튀어 올랐다 / 두 번

**☐ breathe**

5 숨쉬다

I **breathed** / deeply before my exam.
나는 숨쉬었다 / 깊게 시험 전에

**☐ cease**

6 그만두다

The noise **ceased** / at last.
소음이 멈췄다 / 결국

**☐ crash**

7 충돌하다

The car **crashed** / into the wall.
자동차가 충돌했다 / 벽에

## depart
**8** 떠나다, 출발하다

The train **departed** / at 7:10.
기차가 출발했다 / 7시 10분에

## drive
**9** (차량 등이) 달리다, 질주하다

drives    drove    driven

**Drive** / as fast as you can!
질주하라 / 네가 할 수 있는 만큼 빠르게!

## fly
**10** 날다

flies    flew    flown

Most birds **fly** / in a straight line.
대부분 새들은 난다 / 일렬로

## last
**11** 계속되다

The first snow of this year **lasted** / only a few minutes.
올해 첫눈은 지속됐다 / 겨우 몇 분

## lie
**12** 눕다

lies    lay    lain

Tina **lay** down / on the bed.
티나는 누웠다 / 침대에

## run
**13** 달리다

runs    ran    run

He **ran** / along the passage.
그는 달렸다 / 길을 따라서

## ski
**14** 스키를 타다

I love to **ski** / in winter.
난 스키 타는 것을 좋아한다 / 겨울에

## swim
**15** 수영하다

swims    swam    swum

Turtles **swim** / quite fast.
거북이는 수영한다 / 꽤 빠르게

# Mini Test

A 빈칸에 알맞은 단어를 〈보기〉에서 찾아 쓰세요.

1 We _____ when we were little.
우리는 어렸을 때 다퉜다.

2 She can _____ on one foot.
그녀는 한 발로 균형을 잡을 수 있다.

3 She didn't _____ badly.
그녀는 나쁘게 행동하지 않는다.

4 The ball _____ twice.
그 공은 두 번 튀어 올랐다.

5 I _____ deeply before my exam.
나는 시험 전에 깊게 숨쉬었다.

6 The noise _____ at last.
소음은 결국 멈췄다.

7 The car _____ into the wall.
그 차는 벽에 충돌했다.

8 The train _____ at 7:10.
그 기차는 7시 10분에 출발했다.

보기
argued
behave
crashed
bounced
departed
balance
breathed
ceased

B 단어를 알맞게 배열하여 문장을 완성하세요.

1      as fast as      Drive      you can!

2      Most birds      in a straight line.      fly

3      lasted      The first snow of this year      only a few minutes.

4      Tina      on the bed.      lay down

5      He      along the passage.      ran

6      I      in winter.      love to ski

7      swim      quite fast.      Turtles

C 다음 문장에서 동사를 찾아 동그라미하고, 해석을 써 보세요.

**1** Drive as fast as you can!

_____

**2** Most birds fly in a straight line.

_____

**3** The train departed at 7:10.

_____

**4** She can balance on one foot.

_____

**5** Tina lay down on the bed.

_____

**6** The noise ceased at last.

_____

**7** The car crashed into the wall.

_____

**8** The first snow of this year lasted only a few minutes.

_____

**9** I breathed deeply before my exam.

_____

**10** She didn't behave badly.

_____

**11** Turtles swim quite fast.

_____

**12** We argued when we were little.

_____

**13** I love to ski in winter.

_____

**14** He ran along the passage.

_____

**15** The ball bounced twice.

_____

MP3

| | 3인칭/현재 | 과거 | 과거분사 |
|---|---|---|---|

**agree (with)**

1 (사람)에게 동의하다

Do you **agree** / with me?

너는 동의하니 / 나에게?

**agree (on / to)**

2 ~에 동의하다

Everyone **agreed** / on the plan.

모두 동의했다 / 그 계획에

**crack**

3 갈라지다

The wall **cracked** / after the earthquake.

벽은 갈라졌다 / 지진 후에

**disagree**

4 일치하지 않다, 다르다

Your actions **disagree** / with your words.

너의 행동은 다르다 / 너의 말과

**do**   does   did   done

5 충분하다, 적당하다

This backpack will **do** / for you.

이 책가방은 충분할 것이다 / 너에게

**forget**   forgets   forgot   forgotten

6 잊다

I **forgot** / about the meeting.

나는 잊었다 / 그 미팅에 대해

**form**

7 만들어지다, 생기다

Earth **formed** / over 4 billion years ago.

지구는 만들어졌다 / 40억년 전에

### ■ grow
**8** 커지다

grows     grew     grown

The pumpkin **grew** / as big as a house.
호박이 자랐다 / 집만큼 크게

### ☐ help
**9** 돕다, 거들다

I'm ready / to **help**.
나는 준비됐다 / 도울

### ☐ decrease
**10** 감소하다

The birth rate has **decreased** / in the last decade.
출생률이 떨어졌다 / 지난 십 년에

### ☐ increase
**11** 증가하다

Her pain **increased** / suddenly.
그녀의 통증은 증가했다 / 갑자기

### ☐ join
**12** 합쳐지다, 함께 하다

The two roads **join** / at the town.
그 두 도로는 만난다 / 그 마을에서

### ☐ manage
**13** (어려운 가운데) 살아 나가다

She **managed** / by herself.
그녀는 살아갔다 / 그녀 스스로

### ☐ move
**14** 움직이다

Sea lions **moved** / toward the cold wave.
바다사자는 움직였다 / 차가운 파도를 향해

### ☐ listen
**15** 듣다, 귀를 기울이다

You have to **listen** / to others.
너는 들어야 한다 / 다른 사람들에게

# Mini Test

A 빈칸에 알맞은 단어를 〈보기〉에서 찾아 쓰세요.

**1** Do you _____ me?

너는 나에게 동의하니?

**2** Everyone _____ the plan.

모두 그 계획에 동의했다.

**3** The wall _____ after the earthquake.

벽은 지진 후에 갈라졌다.

**4** This backpack will _____ for you.

이 책가방은 너에게 충분할 것이다.

**5** Your actions _____ with your words.

너의 행동들은 너의 말과 다르다.

**6** I _____ about the meeting.

나는 그 미팅에 대해 잊었다.

**7** Earth _____ over 4 billion years ago.

지구는 40억년 전에 만들어졌다.

**8** The pumpkin _____ as big as a house.

호박이 집만큼 크게 자랐다.

보기
disagree
agree with
agreed on
cracked
forgot
do
formed
grew

B 단어를 알맞게 배열하여 문장을 완성하세요.

**1** ready | to help. | I'm

**2** The birth rate | in the last decade. | has decreased

**3** increased | suddenly. | Her pain

**4** The two roads | at the town. | join

**5** managed | She | by herself.

**6** Sea lions | toward the cold wave. | moved

**7** have to listen | You | to others.

C 다음 문장에서 동사를 찾아 동그라미하고, 해석을 써 보세요.

**1** Her pain increased suddenly.

_____

**2** She managed by herself.

_____

**3** You have to listen to others.

_____

**4** The two roads join at the town.

_____

**5** Sea lions moved toward the cold wave.

_____

**6** The birth rate has decreased in the last decade.

_____

**7** The pumpkin grew as big as a house.

_____

**8** I'm ready to help.

_____

**9** Earth formed over 4 billion years ago.

_____

**10** I forgot about the meeting.

_____

**11** This backpack will do for you.

_____

**12** Do you agree with me?

_____

**13** The wall cracked after the earthquake.

_____

**14** Everyone agreed on the plan.

_____

**15** Your actions disagree with your words.

_____

# Day 7

MP3

| | 3인칭/현재 | 과거 | 과거분사 |
|---|---|---|---|

☐ **apologize**

1 사과하다

You should **apologize** / for being late.
너는 사과해야 한다 / 늦은 것을

☐ **assist**

2 돕다

Jamie **assisted** / with making the dinner.
제이미는 도왔다 / 저녁 만드는 것을

☐ **bump**

3 부딪히다

The car **bumped** / into a parked car.
그 차는 부딪쳤다 / 주차된 차에

☐ **call**

4 소리치다, 외치다

She **called** / to people for help.
그녀는 소리쳤다 / 사람들에게 도와달라고

☐ **care**

5 상관하다, 관심을 가지다

We **care** / about children's rights.
우리는 관심을 가진다 / 아이들의 권리에 대해

☐ **consult**

6 상의하다, 의논하다

I **consulted** / with Doctor Kim.
나는 상의했다 / 김 선생님과

☐ **expand**

7 부풀다, 팽창하다

The balloons **expanded**.
그 풍선들은 부풀었다.

## flow
**8** 흐르다

The Han River **flows** / to the sea.
한강은 흐른다 / 바다로

## frown
**9** 눈살을 찌푸리다, 난색을 보이다

Most of us **frown** / on rudeness.
우리 대부분은 눈살을 찌푸린다 / 무례함에

## hurt
**10** 아프다

hurts  hurt  hurt

My back still **hurts**.
등이 여전히 아프다.

## lift
**11** 올라가다; (뚜껑 등이) 열리다

The lid won't **lift**.
그 뚜껑은 열리지 않을 것이다.

## offend
**12** ~에 어긋나다

It can **offend against** the principle of free expressions.
그것은 표현의 자유 원칙에 어긋날 수 있다.

## slide
**13** 미끄러지다

slides  slid  slid

Jack **slid** / down the hill.
잭은 미끄러졌다 / 언덕 아래로

## struggle
**14** 몸부림치다, 힘겹게 나아가다

The rat **struggled** / to escape from the trap.
그 쥐는 몸부림쳤다 / 덫에서 도망치려고

## yell
**15** 소리 지르다

Do not **yell** / in class.
소리 지르지 마라 / 수업 중에

**A** 빈칸에 알맞은 단어를 〈보기〉에서 찾아 쓰세요.

**1** You should _____ for being late.

너는 늦은 것을 사과해야 한다.

**2** Jamie _____ with making the dinner.

제이미는 저녁 만드는 것을 도왔다.

**3** The car _____ into a parked car.

그 차는 주차된 차에 부딪혔다.

**4** She _____ to people for help.

그녀는 사람들에게 도와달라고 소리쳤다.

**5** We _____ about children's rights.

우리는 아이들의 권리에 대해 관심을 가진다.

**6** I _____ with Doctor Kim.

나는 김 선생님과 상의했다.

**7** The balloons _____.

그 풍선들은 팽창했다.

**8** The Han River _____ to the sea.

한강은 바다로 흐른다.

| 보기 |
| --- |
| assisted |
| bumped |
| apologize |
| called |
| expanded |
| flows |
| care |
| consulted |

**B** 단어를 알맞게 배열하여 문장을 완성하세요.

**1** Most of us          on rudeness.          frown

_____

**2**          still hurts.          My back

_____

**3** The lid          lift          won't .

_____

**4** can offend against          It          the principle of free expressions.

_____

**5** slid          Jack          down the hill.

_____

**6** struggled          The rat          to escape from the trap.

_____

**7** Do not          in class.          yell

_____

C 다음 문장에서 동사를 찾아 동그라미하고, 해석을 써 보세요.

**1** The lid won't lift.

_____

**2** Jack slid down the hill.

_____

**3** The car bumped into a parked car.

_____

**4** She called to people for help.

_____

**5** We care about children's rights.

_____

**6** I consulted with Doctor Kim.

_____

**7** The balloons expanded.

_____

**8** The Han River flows to the sea.

_____

**9** Do not yell in class.

_____

**10** My back still hurts.

_____

**11** You should apologize for being late.

_____

**12** It can offend against the principle of free expressions.

_____

**13** Jamie assisted with making the dinner.

_____

**14** The rat struggled to escape from the trap.

_____

**15** Most of us frown on rudeness.

_____

| | 3인칭/현재 | 과거 | 과거분사 |
|---|---|---|---|

**belong**
1  속하다

She **belongs to** the choir club.
그녀는 합창반 소속이다.

**consist**
2  이루어지다, 구성되다

This cookie **consists of** flour, sugar, and butter.
이 쿠키는 밀가루, 설탕, 그리고 버터로 이루어졌다.

**drop**
3  떨어지다

Lisa **dropped** / back to the bed.
리사는 쓰러졌다 / 침대로

**figure**
4  중요하다

The Han River **figures** / greatly in history.
한강은 중요하다 / 역사에서 매우

**glare**
5  노려보다

They **glared** / at each other.
그들은 노려봤다 / 서로를

**happen**
6  발생하다

Many things **happened** / in the last few months.
많은 일이 일어났다 / 지난 몇 달 동안

**joke**
7  농담을 하다

I'm just **joking**.
나는 그냥 농담한 거다.

## perform
**8** 작동하다

The machine **performed** / well.
그 기계는 작동했다 / 잘

## play
**9** 놀다

The kids are **playing** / in the gym.
그 아이들은 놀고 있다 / 실내 체육관에서

## reflect
**10** 심사숙고하다

I have to **reflect** / on myself.
나는 반성해야 한다 / 나 자신을

## draw
**11** 끌다, 모여들다

draws    drew    drawn

The crowd **drew** / back.
군중들이 모여들었다 / 다시

## save
**12** 저축하다

Shoppers can **save** / up to $400 on this laptop.
구매자는 아낄 수 있다 / 400불까지 이 노트북을

## search
**13** 찾다, 탐색하다

The police **searched** / for the missing diamond.
경찰은 탐색했다 / 잃어버린 다이아몬드를

## sigh
**14** 한숨을 쉬다

He **sighed** / with relief.
그는 한숨을 쉬었다 / 안도의

## think
**15** 생각하다

thinks    thought    thought

He couldn't **think** / wisely.
그는 생각할 수 없었다 / 현명하게

39

**A** 빈칸에 알맞은 단어를 〈보기〉에서 찾아 쓰세요.

**1** She _____ to the choir club.

그녀는 합창반 소속이다.

**2** This cookie _____ of flour, sugar, and butter.

이 쿠키는 밀가루, 설탕, 그리고 버터로 이루어졌다.

**3** Lisa _____ back to the bed.

리사는 침대로 쓰러졌다.

**4** The Han River _____ greatly in history.

한강은 역사에서 매우 중요하다.

**5** They _____ at each other.

그들은 서로를 노려봤다.

**6** Many things _____ in the last few months.

많은 일들이 지난 몇 달 동안 일어났다.

**7** I'm just _____.

나는 그냥 농담한 거야.

**8** The machine _____ well.

그 기계는 잘 작동한다.

**B** 단어를 알맞게 배열하여 문장을 완성하세요.

**1**      are playing      The kids      in the gym.

_____

**2**      have to reflect      I      on myself.

_____

**3**      The crowd      back.      drew

_____

**4**      Shoppers      up to $400 on this laptop.      can save

_____

**5**      The police      for the missing diamond.      searched

_____

**6**      with relief.      He      sighed

_____

**7**      He      wisely.      couldn't think

_____

C 다음 문장에서 동사를 찾아 동그라미하고, 해석을 써 보세요.

1 The crowd drew back.

_____

2 The kids are playing in the gym.

_____

3 I'm just joking.

_____

4 I have to reflect on myself.

_____

5 They glared at each other.

_____

6 The police searched for the missing diamond.

_____

7 Lisa dropped back to the bed.

_____

8 He sighed with relief.

_____

9 This cookie consists of flour, sugar, and butter.

_____

10 The Han River figures greatly in history.

_____

11 She belongs to the choir club.

_____

12 He couldn't think wisely.

_____

13 Many things happened in the last few months.

_____

14 The machine performed well.

_____

15 Shoppers can save up to $400 on this laptop.

_____

MP3

| | 3인칭/현재 | 과거 | 과거분사 |
|---|---|---|---|

**contrast**
1    ~과 대조를 이루다

The dark colors **contrasted** / with the pretty pastels.
어두운 색들은 대조를 이뤘다 / 예쁜 파스텔 색들과

**count**
2    의존하다

You can **count on** me.
너는 나에게 기댈 수 있다.

**dip**
3    가라앉다, 떨어지다

The price of oil **dipped** / rapidly.
석유의 가격이 떨어졌다 / 급격하게

**extend**
4    펼쳐지다, 이어지다

The wedding **extended** / over the weekend.
결혼식이 펼쳐졌다 / 주말 동안

**fade**
5    (색이) 바래다, 희미해지다

The colors **faded**.
색깔들이 희미해졌다.

**follow**
6    뒤따라 가다[오다]

She got off the bus, / and I **followed**.
그녀가 버스에서 내렸다 / 그리고 나는 따라갔다

**heat**
7    뜨거워지다

The mug **heated up** / quickly.
그 머그는 뜨거워졌다 / 빠르게

## judge
**8** 판정하다, 판단하다

We shouldn't **judge** / by appearance.
우리는 판단해서는 안 된다 / 외모로

## react
**9** 반응하다

How did your mom **react** / to your test score?
너희 엄마는 어떻게 반응하니 / 네 시험 성적에?

## slip
**10** 미끄러지다

Nari **slipped** / in the hallway.
나리는 미끄러졌다 / 복도에서

## stick
**11** 달라붙다

sticks    sticked/stuck    sticked/stuck

Will this wallpaper **stick** / to the wall?
이 벽지가 붙을까 / 벽에?

## survive
**12** 살아남다

Only she **survived** / out of her family.
그녀만 살아남았다 / 그녀의 가족 중에

## tear
**13** 찢어지다

tears    tore    torn

The book **tears** / easily.
그 책은 찢어진다 / 쉽게

## watch
**14** 보다, 지켜보다

I **watched** / for a while.
나는 지켜봤다 / 한동안

## worry
**15** 걱정하다

I **worried** / about you.
나는 걱정했다 / 너를

# Mini Test

**A** 빈칸에 알맞은 단어를 〈보기〉에서 찾아 쓰세요.

**1** The dark colors _____ with the pretty pastels.

어두운 색들은 예쁜 파스텔 색들과 대조를 이뤘다.

**2** You can _____ on me.

너는 나에게 기댈 수 있다.

**3** The price of oil _____ rapidly.

석유의 가격이 급격하게 떨어졌다.

**4** The wedding _____ over the weekend.

결혼식이 주말 동안 펼쳐졌다.

**5** The colors _____.

색들이 희미해졌다.

**6** She got off the bus, and I _____.

그녀는 버스에서 내렸고 나는 따라갔다.

**7** The mug _____ up quickly.

그 머그는 빠르게 뜨거워졌다.

**8** We shouldn't _____ by appearance.

우리는 외모로 판단해서는 안 되다.

followed
heated
judge
extended
faded
dipped
count
contrasted

**B** 단어를 알맞게 배열하여 문장을 완성하세요.

**1**  to your score?  How did your mom  react

**2**  Nari  in the hallway.  slipped

**3**  Will this wallpaper  to the wall?  stick

**4**  survived  Only she  out of her family.

**5**  The book  easily.  tears

**6**  I  for a while.  watched

**7**  worried  I  about you.

44

C 다음 문장에서 동사를 찾아 동그라미하고, 해석을 써 보세요.

1 Nari slipped in the hallway.
_____

2 How did your mom react to your test score?
_____

3 The book tears easily.
_____

4 I watched for a while.
_____

5 The colors faded.
_____

6 I worried about you.
_____

7 The wedding extended over the weekend.
_____

8 We shouldn't judge by appearance.
_____

9 You can count on me.
_____

10 The dark colors contrasted with the pretty pastels.
_____

11 Will this wallpaper stick to the wall?
_____

12 Only she survived out of her family.
_____

13 The price of oil dipped rapidly.
_____

14 The mug heated up quickly.
_____

15 She got off the bus, and I followed.
_____

| | 3인칭/현재 | 과거 | 과거분사 |
|---|---|---|---|

**□ approve**

1  찬성하다, 괜찮다고 생각하다

My teacher **approved** / of my plan.
우리 선생님은 찬성했다 / 나의 계획에

**□ differ**

2  다르다

Korea and Japan **differ** / in culture.
한국과 일본은 다르다 / 문화가

**□ inquire**

3  문의하다, 묻다

I **inquired** / about a part-time job.
나는 문의했다 / 아르바이트 자리를

**■ learn**

4  배우다, 공부하다

| | learns | learned/<br>learnt | learned/<br>learnt |

You can **learn** / by experience.
너는 배울 수 있다 / 경험을 통해

**□ lock**

5  잠그다, 잠기다, 닫히다

His car door **locked** / automatically.
그의 자동차 문이 잠겼다 / 자동으로

**□ melt**

6  녹다

The snow **melted**.
눈이 녹았다.

**□ mind**

7  주의하다, 조심하다

You'd better **mind** / now.
너는 조심하는 게 좋을 거야 / 지금

## participate
**8** 참여하다

She **participated** / in our discussions.
그녀는 참여했다 / 우리 논의에

## pick
**9** 쪼다, 찍다

The birds **picked** / at the bread.
그 새는 쪼았다 / 빵을

## quit
**10** 그만두다

| quits | quitted/ quit | quitted/ quit |
| --- | --- | --- |

He **quit** / for no reason.
그는 그만뒀다 / 이유 없이

## read
**11** (사람이) 독서하다; (내용이) 쓰여 있다

| reads | read[red] | read[red] |
| --- | --- | --- |

The washing machine's manual **read** / well.
세탁기의 사용설명서가 쓰여 있었다 / 잘

## repeat
**12** 반복되다

**Repeat** / after me.
반복해 / 나를 따라서

## ride
**13** 타다, 타고 가다

| rides | rode | ridden |
| --- | --- | --- |

He **rode** / in a train.
그는 탔다 / 열차에

## shower
**14** 샤워를 하다

You have to **shower** / before and after swimming.
너는 샤워를 해야 한다 / 수영 전후에

## swing
**15** 흔들리다

| swings | swung | swung |
| --- | --- | --- |

The curtain **swung** / in the wind.
커튼이 흔들렸다 / 바람에

## Mini Test

**A** 빈칸에 알맞은 단어를 〈보기〉에서 찾아 쓰세요.

**1** My teacher _____ of my plan.

우리 선생님은 나의 계획에 찬성했다.

**2** Korea and Japan _____ in culture.

한국과 일본은 문화가 다르다.

**3** I _____ about a part-time job.

나는 아르바이트 자리를 문의했다.

**4** You can _____ by experience.

너는 경험을 통해 배울 수 있다.

**5** His car door _____ automatically.

그의 자동차 문이 자동으로 잠겼다.

**6** The snow _____ .

눈은 녹았다.

**7** You'd better _____ now.

너는 지금 조심하는 게 좋을 거야.

**8** She _____ in our discussions.

그녀는 우리의 의논에 참여했다.

> **보기**
> approved
> locked
> differ
> participated
> inquired
> learn
> melted
> mind

**B** 단어를 알맞게 배열하여 문장을 완성하세요.

**1**     picked      The birds      at the bread.

_____

**2**     He      for no reason.      quit

_____

**3**     well.      The washing machine's manual      read

_____

**4**     Repeat      me.      after

_____

**5**     rode      He      in a train.

_____

**6**     You      before and after swimming.      have to shower

_____

**7**     in the wind.      The curtain      swung

_____

C 다음 문장에서 동사를 찾아 동그라미하고, 해석을 써 보세요.

**1** The snow melted.

_____

**2** You'd better mind now.

_____

**3** He quit for no reason.

_____

**4** Repeat after me.

_____

**5** The birds picked at the bread.

_____

**6** I inquired about a part-time job.

_____

**7** You have to shower before and after swimming.

_____

**8** The washing machine's manual read well.

_____

**9** She participated in our discussions.

_____

**10** His car door locked automatically.

_____

**11** He rode in a train.

_____

**12** You can learn by experience.

_____

**13** My teacher approved of my plan.

_____

**14** Korea and Japan differ in culture.

_____

**15** The curtain swung in the wind.

_____

MP3

| | 3인칭/현재 | 과거 | 과거분사 |
|---|---|---|---|

**□ aspire**

1 열망하다

Morgan **aspired** / to become a police officer.
모건은 정말 바란다 / 경찰관이 되기를

**□ count**

2 중요하다

First impressions **count**.
첫인상은 중요하다.

**■ dream**

3 꿈꾸다 | dreams | dreamed/ dreamt | dreamed/ dreamt |

He **dreamt** / of becoming a teacher.
그녀는 꿈꿨다 / 선생님이 되기를

**□ dwell**

4 살다, 거주하다

They **dwell** / in the country.
그들은 거주한다 / 시골에

**□ emerge**

5 (물, 어둠 등에서) 나타나다

A snake **emerged** / from under the car hood.
뱀이 나타났다 / 자동차 후드 아래에서

**□ guess**

6 넘겨짚다, 짐작하여 말하다

I always **guess** / wrong.
나는 항상 짐작한다 / 틀리게

**■ hear**

7 듣다, 소식을 듣다 | hears | heard | heard |

I couldn't **hear** / from my right ear.
나는 들을 수 없었다 / 오른쪽 귀로

50

## hesitate
8   주저하다, 망설이다

They **hesitated** / before leaving the amusement park.
그들은 망설였다 / 놀이동산을 떠나기 전에

## improve
9   좋아지다, 향상하다

She **improved** / in English.
그녀는 향상시켰다 / 영어 실력을

## progress
10   앞으로 나아가다, 진행되다

Katie **progressed** / toward the east gate.
케이티는 나아갔다 / 동문쪽으로

## reply
11   대답하다

Please **reply** / to my letter.
제발 답장해 줘 / 내 편지에

## sail
12   항해하다

They **sailed** / across the open ocean.
그들은 항해했다 / 바다를 가로질러

## see
13   보다     sees     saw     seen

Owls **see** / best at night.
부엉이는 본다 / 밤에 가장 잘

## smile
14   웃다, 미소 짓다

Dora **smiled** / at her daughter.
도라는 웃었다 / 그녀의 딸에게

## vanish
15   사라지다

The magician **vanished** / in a puff of smoke.
마술사는 사라졌다 / 뿜어져 나온 연기 속으로

A 빈칸에 알맞은 단어를 〈보기〉에서 찾아 쓰세요.

**1** Morgan _____ to become a police officer.

모건은 경찰관이 되기를 정말 바란다.

**2** First impressions _____.

첫인상은 중요하다.

**3** He _____ of becoming a teacher.

그녀는 선생님이 되기를 꿈꿨다.

**4** They _____ in the country.

그들은 시골에 살았다.

**5** A snake _____ from under the car hood.

자동차 후드 아래에서 뱀이 나타났다.

**6** I always _____ wrong.

나는 항상 틀리게 짐작한다.

**7** I couldn't _____ from my right ear.

나는 오른쪽 귀로 들을 수 없었다.

**8** They _____ before leaving the amusement park.

그들은 놀이동산을 떠나기 전에 망설였다.

| 보기 |
| --- |
| dwell |
| count |
| aspired |
| dreamt |
| emerged |
| hear |
| guess |
| hesitated |

B 단어를 알맞게 배열하여 문장을 완성하세요.

**1** She | in English. | improved

_____

**2** toward the east gate. | Katie | progressed

_____

**3** to | Please reply | my letter.

_____

**4** sailed | They | across the open ocean.

_____

**5** Owls | best at night. | see

_____

**6** smiled | Dora | at her daughter.

_____

**7** vanished | The magician | in a puff of smoke.

_____

C 다음 문장에서 동사를 찾아 동그라미하고, 해석을 써 보세요.

**1** They sailed across the open ocean.

_____

**2** She improved in English.

_____

**3** The magician vanished in a puff of smoke.

_____

**4** Owls see best at night.

_____

**5** Dora smiled at her daughter.

_____

**6** Please reply to my letter.

_____

**7** Katie progressed toward the east gate.

_____

**8** They dwell in the country.

_____

**9** First impressions count.

_____

**10** He dreamt of becoming a teacher.

_____

**11** I couldn't hear from my right ear.

_____

**12** I always guess wrong.

_____

**13** Morgan aspired to become a police officer.

_____

**14** They hesitated before leaving the amusement park.

_____

**15** A snake emerged from under the car hood.

_____

MP3

| | | 3인칭/현재 | 과거 | 과거분사 |
|---|---|---|---|---|

■ **bet**
1  내기를 하다                    bets        bet         bet

I don't **bet** / on anything.
나는 내기를 하지 않는다 / 어떤 것에도

☐ **charge**
2  지불을 청구하다

The bus company will **charge** / more.
버스 회사는 지불을 청구할 것이다 / 더

☐ **contribute**
3  기부하다, 기여하다

I **contributed** / to my team's success.
나는 기여했다 / 우리 팀의 성공에

■ **deal**
4  다루다                        deals       dealt       dealt

We have **dealt with** the problem about the environment.
우리는 환경에 대한 문제를 다루어 왔다.

☐ **evolve**
5  (점점) 전개되다, 진화하다

Mobile games have **evolved** / rapidly.
모바일 게임은 진화했다 / 빠르게

☐ **gamble**
6  돈을 걸다, 도박을 하다

He **gambles** / at cards.
그는 도박을 한다 / 카드놀이에

■ **lose**
7  실패하다, 손해 보다            loses       lost        lost

The fund manager **lost** / heavily.
펀드 매니저는 손해를 봤다 / 크게

**pause**
8 (잠시) 멈추다

He **paused** / before replying.
그는 멈췄다 / 답변하기 전에

**pay**      pays     paid     paid
9 이익이 되다, 수지가 맞다

His store didn't **pay**.
그의 가게는 수지가 맞지 않았다.

**qualify**
10 자격을 얻다

He **qualified** / as a doctor.
그는 자격을 얻었다 / 의사로

**recover**
11 회복하다, 낫다

She **recovered** / from her injury completely.
그녀는 회복했다 / 그녀의 부상에서 완전히

**settle**
12 합의하다, 정착하다

They **settled** / in New Jersey.
그들은 정착했다 / 뉴저지에

**shut**      shuts     shut     shut
13 닫히다, 잠기다

The lid won't **shut**.
그 뚜껑은 닫히지 않을 것이다.

**sign**
14 서명하다

I **signed** / for a package.
나는 서명했다 / 소포에 대해

**win**      wins     won     won
15 이기다, 승리하다

I often **win** / at cards.
나는 종종 이긴다 / 카드놀이에

**A** 빈칸에 알맞은 단어를 〈보기〉에서 찾아 쓰세요.

**1** I don't _____ on anything.

나는 어떤 것에도 내기를 하지 않는다.

**2** The bus company will _____ more.

버스 회사는 지불을 더 청구할 것이다.

**3** I _____ to my team's success.

나는 우리 팀의 성공에 기여했다.

**4** We have _____ with the problem about the environment.

우리는 환경에 대한 문제를 다루어 왔다.

**5** Mobile games have _____ rapidly.

모바일 게임은 빠르게 진화했다.

**6** He _____ at cards.

그는 카드놀이로 도박을 한다.

**7** The fund manager _____ heavily.

그 펀드 매니저는 크게 손해를 봤다.

**8** He _____ before replying.

그는 답변하기 전에 멈췄다.

| 보기 |
| --- |
| bet |
| dealt |
| evolved |
| paused |
| charge |
| gambles |
| lost |
| contributed |
| paused |

**B** 단어를 알맞게 배열하여 문장을 완성하세요.

**1**  didn't          His store          pay.

_____

**2**  qualified          He          as a doctor.

_____

**3**  recovered          from her injury completely.          She

_____

**4**  settled          They          in New Jersey.

_____

**5**  The lid          shut.          won't

_____

**6**  I          for a package.          signed

_____

**7**  win at cards.          I          often

_____

C 다음 문장에서 동사를 찾아 동그라미하고, 해석을 써 보세요.

**1** His store didn't pay.

_____

**2** I signed for a package.

_____

**3** I contributed to my team's success.

_____

**4** He qualified as a doctor.

_____

**5** I often win at cards.

_____

**6** He gambles at cards.

_____

**7** The lid won't shut.

_____

**8** We have dealt with the problem about the environment.

_____

**9** I don't bet on anything.

_____

**10** He paused before replying.

_____

**11** She recovered from her injury completely.

_____

**12** They settled in New Jersey.

_____

**13** The fund manager lost heavily.

_____

**14** The bus company will charge more.

_____

**15** Mobile games have evolved rapidly.

_____

MP3

| | 3인칭/현재 | 과거 | 과거분사 |
|---|---|---|---|

☐ **insist**
1 주장하다, 우기다, 강조하다

I **insist on** two hours a day / to do nothing.
나는 하루에 두 시간씩 시간을 갖자고 주장한다 / 아무것도 하지 않으면서

☐ **matter**
2 중요하다, 문제되다

It doesn't **matter** / to me.
그것은 중요하지 않다 / 나에게

☐ **resist**
3 저항하다

He can't **resist** / anymore.
그는 저항할 수 없다 / 더 이상

☐ **respond**
4 응답하다

I **responded** / to the survey.
나는 대답했다 / 설문에

☐ **retire**
5 은퇴하다

My mom **retired** / as a doctor.
우리 엄마는 은퇴했다 / 의사로

☐ **return**
6 돌아가다, 돌아오다

They've **returned** / from living abroad.
그들은 돌아왔다 / 외국 생활에서

☐ **start**
7 시작되다

The campaign will **start** / next month.
그 캠페인은 시작할 것이다 / 다음 달에

## subscribe
**8** 구독하다 가입하다

Some families **subscribe to** streaming services.
몇몇 가정은 스트리밍 서비스를 구독한다.

## sympathize
**9** 동정하다, 공감하다

I **sympathize** / with my friends' concerns.
나는 동정한다 / 내 친구들의 고민에

## tend
**10** (~하는) 경향이 있다, (~하기) 쉽다

We **tend** / to make mistakes.
우리는 경향이 있다 / 실수를 만드는

## transfer
**11** (학교 등을) 옮기다, 전학하다

I've **transferred** / to Art school.
나는 예술 학교로 전학했다.

## try
**12** 애쓰다, 노력하다

You must **try** / harder.
너는 시도해야만 한다 / 더 열심히

## turn
**13** 돌다, 회전하다

The car **turned** / to the right.
그 차는 돌았다 / 오른쪽으로

## vote
**14** 투표하다

We have to **vote** / on a bill.
우리는 투표해야 한다 / 법안에

## wake
**15** (잠에서) 깨다

wakes   woke   woken

The baby had **woken** / from a deep sleep.
아기는 깨어났다 / 깊은 잠에서

# Mini Test

**A** 빈칸에 알맞은 단어를 〈보기〉에서 찾아 쓰세요.

**1** I _____ on two hours a day to do nothing.

나는 하루 두 시간 아무것도 안 하기를 주장한다.

**2** It doesn't _____ to me.

그것은 나에게 중요하지 않다.

**3** He can't _____ anymore.

그는 더 이상 저항할 수 없다.

**4** I _____ to the survey.

나는 설문에 대답했다.

**5** My mom _____ as a doctor.

우리 엄마는 의사로 은퇴했다.

**6** They've _____ from living abroad.

그들은 외국 생활에서 돌아왔다.

**7** The campaign will _____ next month.

그 캠페인은 다음 달에 시작할 것이다.

**8** Some families _____ streaming services.

몇몇 가정은 스트리밍 서비스를 구독한다.

〈보기〉
insist
resist
responded
retired
matter
returned
start
subscribe to

**B** 단어를 알맞게 배열하여 문장을 완성하세요.

**1** my friends' concerns.    with    sympathize    I

**2** tend to    We    make mistakes.

**3** I've    to Art school.    transferred

**4** You    harder.    must try

**5** turned    The car    to the right.

**6** have to vote    We    on a bill.

**7** had woken    The baby    from a deep sleep.

C 다음 문장에서 동사를 찾아 동그라미하고, 해석을 써 보세요.

**1** I've transferred to Art school.

_____

**2** It doesn't matter to me.

_____

**3** He can't resist anymore.

_____

**4** I sympathize with my friends' concerns.

_____

**5** My mom retired as a doctor.

_____

**6** Some families subscribe to streaming services.

_____

**7** The car turned to the right.

_____

**8** The baby had woken from a deep sleep.

_____

**9** We tend to make mistakes.

_____

**10** They've returned from living abroad.

_____

**11** You must try harder.

_____

**12** The campaign will start next month.

_____

**13** I responded to the survey.

_____

**14** We have to vote on a bill.

_____

**15** I insist on two hours a day to do nothing.

_____

| | 3인칭/현재 | 과거 | 과거분사 |
|---|---|---|---|

☐ **account**

1 설명하다, 차지하다, 책임지다

He **accounted for** all the team's points in the game.
그는 그 경기에서 팀 점수의 전부를 차지했다.

■ **hang**                 hangs     hung     hung

2 걸리다, 매달리다

The sign was **hanging** / by the entrance.
그 간판은 걸려 있었다 / 입구에

☐ **interpret**

3 통역하다

She **interpreted** / for me.
그녀는 통역했다 / 나를 위해

☐ **look (at)**

4 (~을) 보다

Jina **looked** / at it closely.
지나는 봤다 / 그것을 자세히

☐ **look (for)**

5 (~을) 찾다

I'm **looking** / for my wallet.
나는 찾고 있다 / 내 지갑을

☐ **observe**

6 관찰하다

He **observed** / keenly.
그는 관찰했다 / 날카롭게

☐ **operate**

7 작동하다, 작용하다

The old vacuum **operated** / properly.
낡은 진공청소기는 작동했다 / 제대로

☐ **pour**

**8** 흘러나오다, (비가) 퍼붓다

Rain **poured** / for three days.
비가 퍼부었다 / 사흘 동안

☐ **rain**

**9** 비가 오다

It will **rain** / tomorrow.
비가 올 거다 / 내일

■ **rise**                                 rises          rose          risen

**10** 떠오르다, 오르다

The sun **rises** / in the East.
해가 뜬다 / 동쪽에서

■ **set**                                  sets           set           set

**11** 지다

The sun **set** / at seven yesterday.
해가 졌다 / 어제 7시에

■ **sink**                                 sinks          sank          sunken

**12** 가라앉다

A treasure ship **sank** / in a storm in 1850.
보물선이 가라앉았다 / 1850년에 있었던 폭풍에서

☐ **snow**

**13** 눈이 오다

It has **snowed** / a lot.
눈이 왔다 / 많이

☐ **study**

**14** 공부하다, 배우다

He **studied** / at a Japanese university.
그는 공부했다 / 일본 대학에서

☐ **vary**

**15** 각기 다르다

Actual colors may **vary** / from monitor to monitor.
실제 색상은 다를 수 있다 / 모니터마다

A 빈칸에 알맞은 단어를 〈보기〉에서 찾아 쓰세요.

1 He _____ all the team's points in the game.
   그는 그 경기에서 팀 점수의 전부를 차지했다.

2 The sign was _____ by the entrance.
   그 간판은 입구에 걸려 있었다.

3 She _____ for me.
   그녀는 나를 위해 통역했다.

4 Jina _____ at it closely.
   지나는 그것을 자세히 봤다.

5 I'm _____ for my wallet.
   나는 지갑을 찾고 있다.

6 He _____ keenly.
   그는 날카롭게 관찰했다.

7 The old vacuum _____ properly.
   낡은 진공청소기는 제대로 작동했다.

8 Rain _____ for three days.
   비가 사흘 동안 퍼부었다.

> **보기**
> looked
> accounted for
> hanging
> interpreted
> looking
> observed
> poured
> operated

B 단어를 알맞게 배열하여 문장을 완성하세요.

1 It | tomorrow. | will rain
_____

2 The sun | in the East. | rises
_____

3 at seven yesterday. | The sun | set
_____

4 A treasure ship | in a storm in 1850. | sank
_____

5 has snowed | a lot. | It
_____

6 studied | He | at a Japanese university.
_____

7 from monitor to monitor. | Actual colors | may vary
_____

C 다음 문장에서 동사를 찾아 동그라미하고, 해석을 써 보세요.

1 He accounted for all the team's points in the game.

_____

2 The sign was hanging by the entrance.

_____

3 Jina looked at it closely.

_____

4 A treasure ship sank in a storm in 1850.

_____

5 Actual colors may vary from monitor to monitor.

_____

6 It will rain tomorrow.

_____

7 The sun set at seven yesterday.

_____

8 It has snowed a lot.

_____

9 The sun rises in the East.

_____

10 He observed keenly.

_____

11 Rain poured for three days.

_____

12 I'm looking for my wallet.

_____

13 He studied at a Japanese university.

_____

14 She interpreted for me.

_____

15 The old vacuum operated properly.

_____

| | 3인칭/현재 | 과거 | 과거분사 |
|---|---|---|---|

☐ **rank**

1 자리 잡다

Canada **ranks** / high in business competitiveness.
캐나다는 자리 잡았다 / 비즈니스 경쟁에서 상위에

☐ **reach**

2 뻗다, 미치다, 닿다

Those trees nearly **reach** / to the top of the house.
저 나무들은 거의 닿는다 / 집 꼭대기에

☐ **refer**

3 참고하다, 언급하다

I've **referred to** this book.
나는 이 책을 참고했다.

☐ **rest**

4 휴식을 취하다

We **rested** / from the work.
우리는 휴식을 취했다 / 일로부터

☐ **result**

5 생기다, 발생하다

Many diseases **result from** bad hygiene.
불량한 위생에서 많은 병이 생긴다.

☐ **rush**

6 돌진하다

A car **rushed** / past me.
자동차가 돌진했다 / 나를 지나

■ **shake**          shakes          shook          shaken

7 흔들리다

The leaves **shook** / in the wind.
나뭇잎들이 흔들렸다 / 바람에

□ **shout**
8  외치다

I **shouted** / to Mina to come.
나는 소리쳤다 / 미나에게 오라고

■ **sit**
9  앉다

| sits | sat | sat |

Please **sit down**.
앉으세요.

■ **sleep**
10  자다

| sleeps | slept | slept |

I haven't **slept** / well in weeks.
나는 자지 못했다 / 몇 주 동안 잘

□ **succeed**
11  성공하다

He **succeeded** / in business.
그는 성공했다 / 사업에

□ **suffer**
12  겪다

I often **suffer** / from jet lag.
나는 종종 겪는다 / 시차로 인한 피로를

■ **understand**
13  이해하다, 알다

| understands | understood | understood |

Do you **understand**?
이해하니?

□ **wait**
14  기다리다

**Wait** / for a moment.
기다려 / 잠깐

□ **work**
15  효과가 있다

The pills **worked** / for me.
그 알약은 효과가 있었다 / 나에게

# Mini Test

A 빈칸에 알맞은 단어를 〈보기〉에서 찾아 쓰세요.

**1** Canada _____ high in business competitiveness.

캐나다는 상업 경쟁에서 상위에 자리 잡았다.

**2** Those trees nearly _____ to the top of the house.

저 나무들은 집 꼭대기에 거의 닿는다.

**3** I've _____ this book.

나는 이 책을 참고했다.

**4** We _____ from the work.

우리는 일로부터 휴식을 취했다.

**5** Many diseases _____ bad hygiene.

많은 병이 불량한 위생으로부터 생긴다.

**6** A car _____ past me.

자동차가 나를 지나 돌진했다.

**7** The leaves _____ in the wind.

나뭇잎들이 바람에 흔들렸다.

**8** I _____ to Mina to come.

나는 미나에게 오라고 소리쳤다.

보기
reach
ranks
result from
shook
referred to
rested
shouted
rushed

B 단어를 알맞게 배열하여 문장을 완성하세요.

**1** sit　　Please　　down.

_____

**2** I　　well in weeks.　　haven't slept

_____

**3** succeeded　　He　　in business.

_____

**4** suffer　　I often　　from jet lag.

_____

**5** Do　　understand?　　you

_____

**6** Wait　　a moment.　　for

_____

**7** worked　　The pills　　for me.

_____

68

C 다음 문장에서 동사를 찾아 동그라미하고, 해석을 써 보세요.

**1** He succeeded in business.

_____

**2** Those trees nearly reach to the top of the house.

_____

**3** I haven't slept well in weeks.

_____

**4** We rested from the work.

_____

**5** Do you understand?

_____

**6** Wait for a moment.

_____

**7** The pills worked for me.

_____

**8** I shouted to Mina to come.

_____

**9** The leaves shook in the wind.

_____

**10** I've referred to this book.

_____

**11** Canada ranks high in business competitiveness.

_____

**12** I often suffer from jet lag.

_____

**13** Many diseases result from bad hygiene.

_____

**14** Please sit down.

_____

**15** A car rushed past me.

_____

| | 3인칭/현재 | 과거 | 과거분사 |
|---|---|---|---|

☐ **chat**

1   수다를 떨다

I **chatted** / with my friends.
나는 수다를 떨었다 / 친구들과

☐ **depend**

2   좌우되다, (on) 의존하다, 의지하다

Leaves' color changes **depend** / on temperature.
나뭇잎의 색깔 변화는 좌우된다 / 온도에

■ **dive**   dives   dived/ dove   dived

3   뛰어 들다

The girl **dived** / into the water.
소녀는 뛰어 들었다 / 물에

☐ **explode**

4   폭발하다

My microwave **exploded**.
내 전자레인지가 폭발했다.

☐ **experiment**

5   실험하다

The cosmetic company has **experimented** / on animals.
그 화장품 회사는 실험을 했다 / 동물로

■ **lead**   leads   led   led

6   이어지다

The door **leads** / to a bathroom.
그 문은 연결된다 / 화장실로

☐ **proceed**

7   나아가다

Please **proceed** / to your nearest shelter.
제발 나가세요 / 가장 가까운 피난처로

☐ **rely**

**8** 의지하다, 믿다

You can **rely on** her work.
너는 그녀의 작업을 믿을 수 있다.

☐ **speak**

**9** (~에게) 말하다

I **spoke** / to Laura regarding that.
나는 말했다 / 로라에게 그것에 대해

☐ **stay**

**10** (그대로) 있다, 남다

She **stayed** / at home.
그녀는 머물렀다 / 집에

■ **take place**

**11** 열리다, 개최되다

takes place took place taken place

Classes will **take place** / in room A.
수업들은 열릴 것이다 / 룸 A에서

☐ **talk**

**12** 말하다

This robot can **talk**.
이 로봇은 말할 수 있다.

☐ **touch**

**13** 닿다

Their hands **touched**.
그들의 손이 닿았다.

☐ **travel**

**14** 여행하다

They **travelled** / abroad.
그들은 여행했다 / 해외로

☐ **work**

**15** 일하다

I **worked** / as an apprentice.
나는 일했다 / 견습생으로

71

A 빈칸에 알맞은 단어를 〈보기〉에서 찾아 쓰세요.

1 I _____ with my friends.
   나는 친구들과 수다를 떨었다.

2 Leaves' color changes _____ on temperature.
   나뭇잎의 색깔 변화는 온도에 좌우된다.

3 The girl _____ into the water.
   소녀는 물에 뛰어 들었다.

4 My microwave _____.
   내 전자레인지가 폭발했다.

5 The cosmetic company _____ on animals.
   그 화장품 회사는 동물 실험을 했다.

6 The door _____ to a bathroom.
   그 문은 화장실로 연결된다.

7 Please _____ to your nearest shelter.
   가장 가까운 피난처로 나가세요.

8 You can _____ her work.
   너는 그녀의 작업을 믿을 수 있다.

보기
dived
depend
lead
exploded
experimented
chatted
rely on
proceed

B 단어를 알맞게 배열하여 문장을 완성하세요.

1   spoke to          I          Laura regarding that.

2   She          at home.          stayed

3   will take place          Classes          in room A.

4   talk.          can          This robot

5   Their          touched.          hands

6   They          abroad.          travelled

7   I          as an apprentice.          worked

C 다음 문장에서 동사를 찾아 동그라미하고, 해석을 써 보세요.

1 This robot can talk.

_____

2 Their hands touched.

_____

3 The girl dived into the water.

_____

4 They travelled abroad.

_____

5 She stayed at home.

_____

6 I worked as an apprentice.

_____

7 Please proceed to your nearest shelter.

_____

8 You can rely on her work.

_____

9 I spoke to Laura regarding that.

_____

10 The cosmetic company has experimented on animals.

_____

11 Classes will take place in room A.

_____

12 I chatted with my friends.

_____

13 Leaves' color changes depend on temperature.

_____

14 My microwave exploded.

_____

15 The door leads to a bathroom.

_____

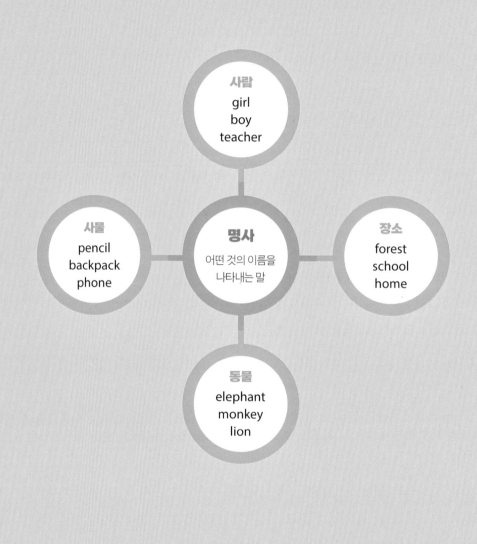

Pattern 02

## 주어 + 동사 + 보어

| 주어 | 동사 | 보어 |
|------|------|------|
| He<br>그는 | is<br>~이다 | a firefighter.<br>소방관 |
| They<br>그들은 | became<br>~이 되었다 | busy.<br>바쁘게 |
| She<br>그는 | remained<br>여전히 ~이었다 | silent.<br>별로 말이 없는 |

is, become, remain 같은 불완전 자동사들은 '주어'와 주어를 '보충해 주는 말(보어)'을 연결해 줘요.

Tip. 불완전 자동사의 보어로 올 수 있는 것들

• 사람이나 사물의 상태를 나타내는 명사류

   Tina   is   an undercover police officer.  티나 = 비밀 경찰

   주어  동사        보어(명사)
   └────── = ──────┘

• 사람이나 사물의 생김새나 상태를 나타내는 형용사류

   Smoothies  are  good for your health. 스무디 = 건강에 좋은

     주어    동사     보어(형용사)
     └────── = ──────┘

MP3

| | 3인칭/현재 | 과거 | 과거분사 |
|---|---|---|---|

### ■ be
**1** (단수) ~이다

is     was     been

She **is** smart.
그녀는 똑똑하다.

\* 1인칭은 am이다.

### ■ be
**2** (복수) ~들이다

are     were     been

Gina and Bory **were** both cute.
지나와 보리는 둘 다 귀여웠다.

### ■ become
**3** ~이 되다

becomes    became    become

The song **became** more and more popular.
그 노래는 점점 유명하게 되었다.

### ■ come
**4** (어떻게) 되다, ~해지다

comes     came     come

Dreams **come** true / when we believe in them.
꿈은 사실이 된다 / 우리가 그것을 믿을 때

### ■ fall
**5** ~해지다

falls     fell     fallen

They **fell** asleep / when the play started.
그들은 잠들었다 / 연극이 시작했을 때

### ■ get
**6** ~이 되다

gets     got     got/gotten

John **got** bored.
존은 지루해 졌다.

### ■ go
**7** ~이 되다

goes     went     gone

This apple **went** bad.
이 사과는 썩었다.

76

### hold
**8** 계속 ~하다

holds    held    held

**Hold** still / while I take your picture.
계속 가만히 있어라 / 내가 사진을 찍을 동안

### keep
**9** 계속 ~한 상태이다

keeps    kept    kept

Tom **kept** silent.
톰은 계속 조용한 상태였다.

### lie
**10** (움직임 없는 상태로) 있다

lies    lay    lain

Snow **lay** thick / on the ground.
눈은 두껍게 있었다 / 땅 위에

### remain
**11** 계속 ~하다

He **remained** calm / under any circumstances.
그는 계속 침착했다 / 어떤 상황에서도

### run
**12** ~이 되다

runs    ran    run

The well **ran** dry.
우물이 말랐다.

### stand
**13** ~한 상태이다

stands    stood    stood

The castle **stood** empty / for a long time.
그 성은 텅 빈 상태였다 / 오랫동안

### stay
**14** 계속 ~하다

You always **stay** indoors.
너는 항상 실내에 있는다.

# Mini Test

**A** 빈칸에 알맞은 단어를 〈보기〉에서 찾아 쓰세요.

**1** She _____ smart.

그녀는 똑똑하다.

**2** Gina and Bory _____ both cute.

지나와 보리는 둘 다 귀여웠다.

**3** The song _____ more and more popular.

그 노래는 점점 유명하게 되었다.

**4** Dreams _____ true when we believe in them.

꿈은 우리가 그것을 믿을 때 사실이 된다.

**5** They _____ asleep when the play started.

그들은 연극이 시작했을 때 잠들었다.

**6** John _____ bored.

존은 지루해 졌다.

**7** This apple _____ bad.

이 사과는 썩었다.

**8** _____ still while I take your picture.

내가 사진을 찍을 동안 계속 가만히 있어라.

보기
fell
were
is
Hold
became
got
went
come

**B** 단어를 알맞게 배열하여 문장을 완성하세요.

**1** kept　　　　　Tom　　　　　silent.

_____

**2** Snow　　　　　thick on the ground.　　　　　lay

_____

**3** He　calm　under any circumstances.　remained

_____

**4** dry.　　　　　The well　　　　　ran

_____

**5** The castle　empty for a long time.　stood

_____

**6** indoors.　　　　　You always　　　　　stay

_____

C 다음 문장에서 동사를 찾아 동그라미하고, 해석을 써 보세요.

**1** Snow lay thick on the ground.

_____

**2** You always stay indoors.

_____

**3** The well ran dry.

_____

**4** John got bored.

_____

**5** They fell asleep when the play started.

_____

**6** Tom kept silent.

_____

**7** This apple went bad.

_____

**8** Hold still while I take your picture.

_____

**9** The castle stood empty for a long time.

_____

**10** Gina and Bory were both cute.

_____

**11** She is smart.

_____

**12** The song became more and more popular.

_____

**13** Dreams come true when we believe in them.

_____

**14** He remained calm under any circumstances.

_____

MP3

| | 3인칭/현재 | 과거 | 과거분사 |
|---|---|---|---|

**act**
1 ~처럼 행동하다

He **acted** dumb / this morning.
그는 바보처럼 행동했다 / 오늘 아침

**appear**
2 ~인 것 같다

She **appeared** unsatisfied / with the result.
그녀는 불만족스러운 것 같았다 / 그 결과에

**feel**   feels   felt   felt
3 ~한 느낌이 들다

He **felt** happy / when he saw Naomi.
그는 행복한 느낌이 들었다 / 그가 나오미를 봤을 때

**grow**   grows   grew   grown
4 점점 ~이 되다

Her grandpa **grew** more and more weak.
그녀의 할아버지는 점점 약하게 됐다.

**look**
5 ~하게 보이다

You **look** happy.
넌 행복해 보인다.

**measure**
6 (길이 등이) ~이다

The tree **measures** 120 centimeters tall.
그 나무는 120 센티미터이다.

**prove**
7 ~임을 증명하다

Building a house **proved** difficult / for us.
집을 짓는 것은 어려운 일임을 증명했다 / 우리에게

**seem**

8 ~인 것 같다

She **seems** nice.
그녀는 착해 보인다.

**smell**

9 ~한 냄새가 나다

It **smells** good.
그것은 좋은 냄새가 난다.

**sound**

10 ~하게 들리다

It **sounds** great.
그것은 좋게 들린다.

**taste**

11 ~한 맛이 나다

It **tastes** delicious.
그것은 맛있다.

**turn**

12 ~으로 변하다

My grandma's hair **turned** grey.
우리 할머니의 머리카락이 백발로 변했다.

**turn out**

13 ~으로 판명 나다

She **turned out** to be a teacher.
그녀는 선생님으로 판명 났다.

A 빈칸에 알맞은 단어를 〈보기〉에서 찾아 쓰세요.

**1** He _____ dumb this morning.

그는 오늘 아침 바보처럼 행동했다.

**2** She _____ unsatisfied with the result.

그녀는 그 결과에 불만족스러운 것 같았다.

**3** He _____ happy when he saw Naomi.

그는 나오미를 봤을 때 행복한 느낌이 들었다.

**4** Her grandpa _____ more and more weak.

그녀의 할아버지는 점점 약하게 됐다.

**5** You _____ happy.

넌 행복해 보인다.

**6** The tree _____ 120 centimeters tall.

그 나무는 120 센티미터이다.

**7** Building a house _____ difficult for us.

집을 짓는 것은 우리에게 어려운 일임을 증명했다.

보기

acted
grew
appeared
felt
look
measures
proved

B 단어를 알맞게 배열하여 문장을 완성하세요.

**1** She    nice.    seems

_____

**2** smells    It    good.

_____

**3** sounds    great.    It

_____

**4** It    delicious.    tastes

_____

**5** My grandma's hair    grey.    turned

_____

**6** She    to be a teacher.    turned out

_____

C 다음 문장에서 동사를 찾아 동그라미하고, 해석을 써 보세요.

**1** It tastes delicious.

_____

**2** You look happy.

_____

**3** She seems nice.

_____

**4** She turned out to be a teacher.

_____

**5** Her grandpa grew more and more weak.

_____

**6** The tree measures 120 centimeters tall.

_____

**7** Building a house proved difficult for us.

_____

**8** It sounds great.

_____

**9** He felt happy when he saw Naomi.

_____

**10** It smells good.

_____

**11** She appeared unsatisfied with the result.

_____

**12** My grandma's hair turned grey.

_____

**13** He acted dumb this morning.

_____

형용사가 있으면

I am a **big** man.
I am **strong**.

형용사가 없으면

I am a big man.
I am strong.

Pattern **3**

## 주어 + 동사 + 목적어

| 주어 | 동사 | 목적어 | |
|------|------|--------|---|
| I<br>나는 | caught<br>~을 잡았다 | a cat.<br>고양이를 | |
| The cat<br>그 고양이는 | has<br>~을 가지고 있다 | a scar<br>흉터를 | on the back.<br>등에 |
| It<br>그것은 | survived<br>살아남았다 | the car accident.<br>자동차 사고에서 | |

타동사 catch는 '~을 잡다'라는 뜻으로 「~을」에 해당하는 '목적어'가 있어야 완전한 의미의 문장을 만들 수 있어요. 영어 동사의 대부분이 타동사여서 공부할 양이 많아요. 하지만 천천히 그리고 꾸준하게 알아가다 보면 영어 완전 정복의 고지가 보일 거예요.

### Tip. 목적어가 될 수 있는 것들

| | | |
|---|---|---|
| **1 명사** | An old man sold <u>fruits</u>. | 한 노인이 과일을 팔았다. |
| **2 대명사** | I found <u>it</u> under the table. | 나는 탁자 아래에서 그것을 발견했다. |
| **3 to + 동사원형** | She wanted <u>to become a doctor</u>. | 그녀는 의사가 되기를 원했다. |
| **4 동사원형 + ing** | He finished <u>doing his homework</u>. | 그는 숙제 하기를 끝냈다. |
| **5 that + 주어 + 동사** | He knows <u>that we passed the test</u>. | 그는 우리가 그 시험에 통과할 것을 안다. |

| | 3인칭/현재 | 과거 | 과거분사 |
|---|---|---|---|

☐ **approach**

1 ~에 다가가다; 접근하다

The bus **approached** the tunnel.
그 버스는 터널에 다가갔다.

☐ **astonish**

2 깜짝 놀라게 하다

Emma **astonished** her family / by winning an award.
엠마는 그녀의 가족을 깜짝 놀라게 했다 / 상을 타서

☐ **confess**

3 ~을 인정하다, 고백하다

Lucy **confessed** that she told a lie.
루시는 그녀가 거짓말을 했다는 것을 고백했다.

☐ **defend**

4 ~을 방어하다, 지키다, 수비하다

General Lee **defended** his country / against enemies.
이 장군은 그의 나라를 지켰다 / 적에 맞서

☐ **explain**

5 ~을 설명하다, 해명하다

My teacher **explains** math / really well.
우리 선생님은 수학을 설명한다 / 매우 잘

☐ **finish**

6 끝내다, 마치다

Have you **finished** your homework / yet?
너는 숙제를 안 끝냈니 / 아직?

☐ **judge**

7 판결을 내리다, 판단하다

Don't **judge** me / by my accent!
날 판단하지 마 / 내 억양으로!

## keep
**8** ~을 가지고 있다

| | keeps | kept | kept |
| --- | --- | --- | --- |

He **kept** the change.
그는 잔돈을 가졌다.

## learn
**9** ~을 배우다, 공부하다

| | learns | learned/ learnt | learned/ learnt |
| --- | --- | --- | --- |

I've **learned** English / since I was a kid.
나는 영어를 배워 왔다 / 내가 어렸을 때부터

## open
**10** ~을 열다

He **opened** the door / for me.
그는 문을 열었다 / 나를 위해

## pause
**11** ~을 정지시키다

Tina **paused** the music / to listen to her mom.
티나는 음악을 정지시켰다 / 엄마의 말을 들으려고

## pay
**12** (임금)을 지불하다, 갚다, 계산하다

| | pays | paid | paid |
| --- | --- | --- | --- |

You have to **pay** your debt.
너는 네 빚을 갚아야만 한다.

## perform
**13** ~을 행하다, 공연하다

Beyonce **performed** a new song / for the audience.
비욘세는 새로운 노래를 공연했다 / 관객들에게

## serve
**14** ~을 위하여 일하다, 음식을 차려주다

I'm honored to **serve** you.
당신들을 위해 일하는 것은 영광이다.

## wrap
**15** ~을 싸다, 포장하다

Please **wrap** the Christmas present / with a nice ribbon.
크리스마스 선물을 포장해 주세요 / 멋진 리본으로

A 빈칸에 알맞은 단어를 〈보기〉에서 찾아 쓰세요.

**1** The bus _____ the tunnel.

그 버스는 터널에 다가갔다.

**2** Emma _____ her family by winning an award.

엠마는 상을 타서 그녀의 가족을 깜짝 놀라게 했다.

**3** Lucy _____ that she told a lie.

루시는 그녀가 거짓말을 했다는 것을 고백했다.

**4** General Lee _____ his country against enemies.

이 장군은 적에 맞서 그의 나라를 지켰다.

**5** My teacher _____ math really well.

우리 선생님은 수학을 매우 잘 설명한다.

**6** Have you _____ your homework yet?

너는 숙제를 아직 안 끝냈니?

**7** Don't _____ me by my accent!

내 억양으로 날 판단하지 마!

**8** He _____ the change.

그는 잔돈을 가졌다.

〈보기〉
defended
astonished
confessed
approached
explains
finished
kept
judge

B 단어를 알맞게 배열하여 문장을 완성하세요.

**1** learned English / since I was a kid. / I've

_____

**2** He / the door for me. / opened

_____

**3** Tina / to listen to her mom. / the music / paused

_____

**4** have to pay / You / your debt.

_____

**5** Beyonce / a new song / for the audience. / performed

_____

**6** to serve / I'm honored / you.

_____

**7** the Christmas present / Please wrap / with a nice ribbon.

_____

C 다음 문장에서 동사를 찾아 동그라미하고, 해석을 써 보세요.

1 Don't judge me by my accent!

_____

2 I've learned English since I was a kid.

_____

3 I'm honored to serve you.

_____

4 He kept the change.

_____

5 Tina paused the music to listen to her mom.

_____

6 Please wrap the Christmas present with a nice ribbon.

_____

7 Beyonce performed a new song for the audience.

_____

8 You have to pay your debt.

_____

9 My teacher explains math really well.

_____

10 The bus approached the tunnel.

_____

11 Have you finished your homework yet?

_____

12 He opened the door for me.

_____

13 Emma astonished her family by winning an award.

_____

14 General Lee defended his country against enemies.

_____

15 Lucy confessed that she told a lie.

_____

MP3

| | 3인칭/현재 | 과거 | 과거분사 |
|---|---|---|---|

☐ **answer**

1 ~에 대답하다

He didn't **answer** my question.
그는 나의 질문에 대답하지 않았다.

☐ **bake**

2 ~을 굽다

We **bake** a turkey / for Thanksgiving dinner.
우리는 칠면조를 굽는다 / 추수감사절 저녁을 위해

☐ **chase**

3 ~을 뒤쫓다

A dog **chased** a hen / around the barn.
개가 닭을 쫓았다 / 헛간 주위에서

☐ **defeat**

4 ~을 격퇴하다, 이기다

Noma **defeated** Sharon / in the student presidential election.
노마는 샤론을 이겼다 / 학생 회장 선거에서

☐ **enroll**

5 ~를 등록하다

He **enrolled** new members.
그는 새로운 회원들을 등록했다.

☐ **expect**

6 ~을 기대하다, 예상하다

We are **expecting** fifty guests / at the party.
우리는 오십 명의 손님을 기대하고 있다 / 파티에

☐ **fit**

7 ~에 맞다, 적합하다, 맞게 하다

Your new jacket **fits** you / well.
네 새 자켓은 너에게 맞는다 / 잘

☐ **join**

8    ~을 연결하다, 합류하다, 가입하다

Minho will **join** the new drama / in March next year.

민호는 새 드라마에 합류할 것이다 / 내년 3월에

☐ **lift**

9    ~을 들어 올리다

He **lifted** his arm / into the air.

그는 자신의 팔을 들어 올렸다 / 허공으로

☐ **order**

10    ~을 명령하다, 주문하다

The captain **ordered** an advance.

대장은 전진을 명령했다.

☐ **owe**

11    ~에 빚이 있다

He **owes** me / over one thousand won.

그는 나에게 빚이 있다 / 천 원 넘게

☐ **pack**

12    (짐을) 싸다, 포장하다

Did you **pack** your bag / for the field trip?

너는 가방을 쌌니 / 소풍을 위해?

☐ **plan**

13    ~을 계획하다

She **planned** a trip / to Thailand.

그녀는 여행을 계획했다 / 태국으로

■ **send**

14    ~을 보내다      sends      sent      sent

She **sent** the parcel / by FedEx.

그녀는 소포를 보냈다 / 페덱스로

☐ **wipe**

15    ~을 닦다

He **wiped** the dirt / from the table.

그는 먼지를 닦았다 / 식탁의

A 빈칸에 알맞은 단어를 〈보기〉에서 찾아 쓰세요.

**1** He didn't _____ my question.

그는 나의 질문에 대답하지 않았다.

**2** We _____ a turkey for Thanksgiving dinner.

우리는 추수감사절 저녁을 위해 칠면조를 굽는다.

**3** A dog _____ a hen around the barn.

개가 헛간 주위에서 닭을 쫓았다.

**4** Noma _____ Sharon in the student presidential election.

노마는 학생 회장 선거에서 샤론을 이겼다.

**5** He _____ new members.

그는 새로운 회원들을 등록했다.

**6** We are _____ fifty guests at the party.

우리는 파티에 오십 명의 손님을 기대하고 있다.

**7** Your new jacket _____ you well.

네 새 자켓은 너에게 잘 맞는다.

**8** Minho will _____ the new drama in March next year.

민호는 내년 3월에 새 드라마에 합류할 것이다.

보기
bake
chased
answer
fits
defeated
enrolled
expecting
join

B 단어를 알맞게 배열하여 문장을 완성하세요.

**1** He        his arm        into the air.        lifted

_____

**2** The captain        an advance.        ordered

_____

**3** owes        me        He        over one thousand won.

_____

**4** your bag        Did you pack        for the field trip?

_____

**5** planned        She        a trip to Thailand.

_____

**6** She        the parcel        by FedEx.        sent

_____

**7** wiped        the dirt        He        from the table.

_____

C 다음 문장에서 동사를 찾아 동그라미하고, 해석을 써 보세요.

1 Your new jacket fits you well.
_____

2 The captain ordered an advance.
_____

3 He wiped the dirt from the table.
_____

4 Minho will join the new drama in March next year.
_____

5 Did you pack your bag for the field trip?
_____

6 We are expecting fifty guests at the party.
_____

7 A dog chased a hen around the barn.
_____

8 He owes me over one thousand won.
_____

9 He lifted his arm into the air.
_____

10 He didn't answer my question.
_____

11 She sent the parcel by FedEx.
_____

12 She planned a trip to Thailand.
_____

13 He enrolled new members.
_____

14 Noma defeated Sharon in the student presidential election.
_____

15 We bake a turkey for Thanksgiving dinner.
_____

MP3

| | 3인칭/현재 | 과거 | 과거분사 |
|---|---|---|---|

**allow**

1  ~을 허락하다

My teacher didn't **allow** snacks / in the classroom.
우리 선생님은 간식 먹는 것을 허락하지 않았다 / 교실에서

**blink**

2  (눈을) 깜박이다

He **blinked** his eyes / nervously.
그는 눈을 깜박였다 / 초조하게

**capture**

3  ~을 붙잡다, 체포하다

The police **captured** the gorilla / that had escaped from the zoo.
경찰은 고릴라를 붙잡았다 / 동물원에서 탈출한

**charm**

4  ~를 매혹하다

Jacob **charmed** audiences / in the speech contest.
제이콥은 관중을 사로잡았다 / 말하기 대회에서

**decrease**

5  ~을 줄이다, 감소시키다

They **decreased** the number of buses.
그들은 버스의 수를 감소시켰다.

**determine**

6  (원인 등)을 알아내다; 결정짓다

Your efforts **determine** your future.
네 노력이 네 미래를 결정한다.

**expand**

7  ~을 펴다, 확대시키다

Heat **expands** air / inside a bottle.
열이 공기를 확대시킨다 / 병 안의

## load
**8** ~에 짐을 싣다

They **loaded** a ship / with cars.
그들은 배에 짐을 실었다 / 자동차로

## lose
**9** ~을 잃다, 잃어버리다

loses    lost    lost

He **lost** his backpack / while playing basketball.
그는 그의 책가방을 잃어버렸다 / 농구를 하는 동안

## oppose
**10** ~을 반대하다

We **oppose** the new megastore opening / in our town.
우리는 새로운 초대형 상점 개점을 반대한다 / 우리 마을에

## organize
**11** ~을 준비하다, 조직하다, 체계화하다

We're going to **organize** a graduation ceremony.
우리는 졸업식을 준비할 것이다.

## play
**12** (게임 등)을 하다

We **play** soccer / every day after school.
우리는 축구를 한다 / 매일 방과 후

## sell
**13** ~을 팔다

sells    sold    sold

Alana **sold** the watch / at a good price.
엘레나는 시계를 팔았다 / 좋은 가격에

## wash
**14** ~을 씻다

She **washed** her face.
그녀는 자신의 얼굴을 씻었다.

## write
**15** ~을 쓰다

writes    wrote    written

I **wrote** an essay / about myself.
나는 에세이를 썼다 / 나 자신에 대해서

A 빈칸에 알맞은 단어를 〈보기〉에서 찾아 쓰세요.

1 My teacher didn't _____ snacks in the classroom.

우리 선생님은 교실에서 과자 먹는 것을 허락하지 않았다.

2 He _____ his eyes nervously.

그는 초조하게 눈을 깜박였다.

3 The police _____ the gorilla that had escaped from the zoo.

경찰은 동물원에서 탈출한 고릴라를 붙잡았다.

4 Jacob _____ audiences in the speech contest.

제이콥은 말하기 대회에서 관중을 사로잡았다.

5 They _____ the number of buses.

그들은 버스의 수를 줄였다.

6 Your efforts _____ your future.

네 노력이 네 미래를 결정한다.

7 Heat _____ air inside a bottle.

열이 병 안의 공기를 확대시킨다.

8 They _____ a ship with cars.

그들은 자동차를 배에 실었다.

| 보기 |
| --- |
| captured |
| expands |
| charmed |
| loaded |
| allow |
| decreased |
| determine |
| blinked |

B 단어를 알맞게 배열하여 문장을 완성하세요.

1 He        while playing basketball.        lost        his backpack

_____

2 We        oppose        in our town.        the new megastore opening

_____

3 We're        a graduation ceremony.        going to organize

_____

4 soccer        We        play        every day after school.

_____

5 Alana        at a good price.        sold        the watch

_____

6 She        her face.        washed

_____

7 I        wrote        about myself.        an essay

_____

C 다음 문장에서 동사를 찾아 동그라미하고, 해석을 써 보세요.

**1** I wrote an essay about myself.
_____

**2** Heat expands air inside a bottle.
_____

**3** We play soccer every day after school.
_____

**4** She washed her face.
_____

**5** We oppose the new megastore opening in our town.
_____

**6** He lost his backpack while playing basketball.
_____

**7** Alana sold the watch at a good price.
_____

**8** He blinked his eyes nervously.
_____

**9** They loaded a ship with cars.
_____

**10** Your efforts determine your future.
_____

**11** They decreased the number of buses.
_____

**12** We're going to organize a graduation ceremony.
_____

**13** My teacher didn't allow snacks in the classroom.
_____

**14** Jacob charmed audiences in the speech contest.
_____

**15** The police captured the gorilla that had escaped from the zoo.
_____

MP3

| | 3인칭/현재 | 과거 | 과거분사 |
|---|---|---|---|

□ **ask**

1 ~에게 묻다, 물어보다

I **asked** people / in the room.
나는 사람들에게 물어봤다 / 방 안

□ **bribe**

2 ~에게 뇌물을 주다

He **bribed** the referee / before his game.
그는 심판에게 뇌물을 줬다 / 자신의 경기 전

■ **buy**      buys     bought     bought

3 ~을 사다

Dylan **bought** a gift / for his brother.
딜란은 선물을 샀다 / 자신의 형을 위해

□ **celebrate**

4 ~을 축하하다

We **celebrated** my birthday / at a fancy restaurant.
우리는 내 생일을 축하했다 / 멋진 레스토랑에서

□ **decline**

5 ~을 거절하다, 사양하다; 기울이다

I **declined** the interview / via email.
나는 인터뷰를 거절했다 / 이메일을 통해

□ **introduce**

6 ~을 소개하다

Let me **introduce** my friend, Hena.
내 친구 헤나를 소개할게.

□ **lack**

7 ~이 부족하다

We **lacked** courage / to ride a roller coaster.
우리는 용기가 부족했다 / 청룡열차를 탈

## manage
**8** ~을 해내다; 경영하다

She **managed** the mission / alone.
그녀는 임무를 해냈다 / 혼자

## obey
**9** ~이 시키는 대로 하다, ~을 따르다

Drivers should **obey** the sign.
운전자는 표지판을 따라야 한다.

## offend
**10** ~의 기분을 상하게 하다

His rude behavior **offended** everybody.
그의 예의 없는 행동이 모두의 기분을 상하게 했다.

## post
**11** (우편물)을 발송하다

She **posted** the card / to Jim.
그녀는 엽서를 부쳤다 / 짐에게

## select
**12** ~을 고르다, 선택하다

The team will **select** a new player / next month.
팀은 새 선수를 고를 것이다 / 다음 달

## test
**13** ~를 시험하다

My teacher **tests** our vocabulary / in every class.
우리 선생님은 어휘를 시험한다 / 매 수업마다

## trick
**14** ~를 속이다, 속임수를 쓰다

They **tricked** their teacher.
그들은 선생님을 속였다.

## worry
**15** ~를 걱정시키다

Don't **worry** me.
나를 걱정시키지 마라.

A 빈칸에 알맞은 단어를 〈보기〉에서 찾아 쓰세요.

1 I _____ people in the room.

나는 방 안 사람들에게 물어봤다.

2 He _____ the referee before his game.

그는 자신의 경기 전에 심판에게 뇌물을 줬다.

3 Dylan _____ a gift for his brother.

딜란은 자신의 형을 위해 선물을 샀다.

4 We _____ my birthday at a fancy restaurant.

우리는 멋진 레스토랑에서 내 생일을 축하했다.

5 I _____ the interview via email.

나는 이메일을 통해 인터뷰를 거절했다.

6 Let me _____ my friend, Hena.

내 친구 헤나를 소개할게.

7 We _____ courage to ride a roller coaster.

우리는 청룡열차를 탈 용기가 부족했다.

8 She _____ the mission alone.

그녀는 혼자 임무를 해냈다.

| 보기 |
|------|
| asked |
| celebrated |
| bribed |
| bought |
| declined |
| lacked |
| introduce |
| managed |

B 단어를 알맞게 배열하여 문장을 완성하세요.

1    Drivers          the sign.          should obey

_____

2    offended     His rude behavior     everybody.

_____

3    posted     the card     She     to Jim.

_____

4    The team     a new player     next month.     will select

_____

5    tests     our vocabulary     in every class.     My teacher

_____

6    tricked     They     their teacher.

_____

7    worry     Don't     me.

_____

C 다음 문장에서 동사를 찾아 동그라미하고, 해석을 써 보세요.

**1** They tricked their teacher.

_____

**2** Don't worry me.

_____

**3** She posted the card to Jim.

_____

**4** He bribed the referee before his game.

_____

**5** I declined the interview via email.

_____

**6** His rude behavior offended everybody.

_____

**7** She managed the mission alone.

_____

**8** We lacked courage to ride a roller coaster.

_____

**9** Drivers should obey the sign.

_____

**10** Let me introduce my friend, Hena.

_____

**11** My teacher tests our vocabulary in every class.

_____

**12** The team will select a new player next month.

_____

**13** Dylan bought a gift for his brother.

_____

**14** I asked people in the room.

_____

**15** We celebrated my birthday at a fancy restaurant.

_____

MP3

| | 3인칭/현재 | 과거 | 과거분사 |
|---|---|---|---|

**attempt**
1 ~을 시도하다

Patrick **attempted** a more difficult question.
패트릭은 더 어려운 질문을 시도했다.

**build**
2 (건물)을 짓다     builds     built     built

The ancient Egyptians **built** the three pyramids of Giza.
고대 이집트인들은 세 개의 피라미드를 기자에 지었다.

**cease**
3 ~을 그만두다

The baby hasn't **ceased** crying / since this morning.
그 아기는 울음을 그치지 않았다 / 오늘 아침부터

**chew**
4 (음식)을 씹다, 깨물다

People often **chew** gum / as a snack.
사람들은 종종 껌을 씹는다 / 간식으로

**decide**
5 ~을 결정하다, 결심하다

I **decided** not to buy a new cell phone.
나는 새 휴대전화기를 사지 않기로 결정했다.

**exercise**
6 ~을 운동시키다, 연습시키다

She **exercised** her dogs / before breakfast.
그녀는 자신의 개를 운동시켰다 / 아침식사 전에

**interpret**
7 ~을 해석하다, 통역하다

Mrs. Cho **interpreted** the speech / into Korean.
조 선생님은 연설문을 해석했다 / 한국어로

## lock
**8** ~을 잠그다

I had **locked** the door / to my bedroom.
나는 문을 잠궜다 / 내 침실로 가는

## mark
**9** ~을 표시하다

They **marked** a door / with a star.
그들은 문에 표시했다 / 별로

## melt
**10** ~을 녹이다

The warm weather **melted** the snow.
따뜻한 날씨가 눈을 녹였다.

## put
**11** ~을 놓다, 두다, 가져가다

puts    put    put

I always **put** my phone / on the desk.
나는 항상 휴대 전화기를 둔다 / 책상 위에

## seek
**12** ~을 찾다, 추구하다

seeks    sought    sought

The man has **sought** the truth / all of his life.
그 남자는 진실을 추구했다 / 그의 평생을

## toss
**13** ~을 던지다

A boy **tossed** a ball / to Mia.
소년이 공을 던졌다 / 미아에게

## win
**14** ~에서 이기다, 승리하다

wins    won    won

My team **won** the race.
우리 팀이 경주에서 이겼다.

## wish
**15** ~이면 좋겠다고 생각하다, 바라다

I **wish** you would come.
나는 네가 오기를 바란다.

# Mini Test

**A** 빈칸에 알맞은 단어를 〈보기〉에서 찾아 쓰세요.

**1** Patrick _____ a more difficult question.

패트릭은 더 어려운 질문을 시도했다.

**2** The ancient Egyptians _____ the three pyramids of Giza.

고대 이집트인들은 세 개의 피라미드를 기자에 지었다.

**3** The baby hasn't _____ crying since this morning.

그 아기는 오늘 아침부터 울음을 그치지 않았다.

**4** People often _____ gum as a snack.

사람들은 종종 간식으로 껌을 씹는다.

**5** I _____ not to buy a new cell phone.

나는 새 휴대전화기를 사지 않기로 결정했다.

**6** She _____ her dogs before breakfast.

그녀는 아침식사 전에 자신의 개를 운동시켰다.

**7** Mrs. Cho _____ the speech into Korean.

조 선생님은 연설문을 한국어로 해석했다.

**8** I had _____ the door to my bedroom.

나는 내 침실로 가는 문을 잠궜다.

보기

attempted
decided
exercised
chew
locked
interpreted
built
ceased

**B** 단어를 알맞게 배열하여 문장을 완성하세요.

**1** They / a door / marked / with a star.

**2** The warm weather / the snow. / melted

**3** I / my phone / put / on the desk.

**4** has sought / The man / the truth / all of his life.

**5** A boy / tossed / to Mia. / a ball

**6** My team / the race. / won

**7** I / you would come. / wish

C 다음 문장에서 동사를 찾아 동그라미하고, 해석을 써 보세요.

**1** I wish you would come.

_____

**2** My team won the race.

_____

**3** A boy tossed a ball to Mia.

_____

**4** I always put my phone on the desk.

_____

**5** The man has sought the truth all of his life.

_____

**6** They marked a door with a star.

_____

**7** The warm weather melted the snow.

_____

**8** I had locked the door to my bedroom.

_____

**9** Mrs. Cho interpreted the speech into Korean.

_____

**10** She exercised her dogs before breakfast.

_____

**11** I decided not to buy a new cell phone.

_____

**12** People often chew gum as a snack.

_____

**13** The baby hasn't ceased crying since this morning.

_____

**14** The ancient Egyptians built the three pyramids of Giza.

_____

**15** Patrick attempted a more difficult question.

_____

MP3

| | 3인칭/현재 | 과거 | 과거분사 |
|---|---|---|---|

## ■ become
1   ~이 알맞다, 어울리다    becomes   became   become

That black suit really **becomes** you.
검정 양복이 너와 정말 어울린다.

## ☐ carve
2   ~을 조각하다, 새기다

The sculptor **carved** a wonderful statue / out of marble.
조각가는 멋진 조각상을 조각했다 / 대리석으로

## ☐ congratulate
3   ~을 축하하다

They **congratulated** Bob / on his Nobel Prize win.
그들은 밥을 축하했다 / 그의 노벨상 수상에

## ☐ debate
4   (문제 등)을 토론하다, 논의하다

They **debated** the matter of free will.
그들은 자유 의지의 문제를 논의했다.

## ☐ define
5   (뜻)을 정의하다, 분명히 밝히다

Your behavior **defines** who you are.
너의 행동은 네가 누구인지 정의한다.

## ☐ exclude
6   ~을 제외하다, 거부하다, 추방하다

The judges **excluded** the key piece of evidence / in this case.
판사는 중요한 증거를 제외했다 / 이 사건에서

## ☐ inform
7   ~을 알리다, 통지하다

The principal **informed** the students / about the new tests.
교장선생님은 학생들에게 알렸다 / 새 시험에 대해

**leak**
**8** (액체, 기체)가 새게 하다

The pipe **leaks** water.
그 관은 물이 샌다.

**lean**
**9** ~을 ~에 기대 놓다

| leans | leaned/ leant | leaned/ leant |
|---|---|---|

She **leaned** her head / on the window.
그녀는 자신의 머리를 기대었다 / 창문에

**marry**
**10** ~와 결혼하다

My sister **married** a Chinese man.
우리 언니는 중국인과 결혼했다.

**mount**
**11** ~에 오르다

The rider **mounted** her horse.
기수가 자신의 말에 올랐다.

**search**
**12** ~을 살펴보다, 찾다

I **searched** my pocket / for money.
나는 내 주머니를 살펴봤다 / 돈을 찾으려고

**suggest**
**13** ~을 제안하다

Mia **suggested** that I go see a doctor.
미아는 내가 병원에 가는 게 좋겠다고 말했다.

**tear**
**14** ~을 찢다, 뜯다

| tears | tore | torn |
|---|---|---|

People **tore** the posters / off the wall.
사람들은 포스터들을 찢었다 / 벽에서

**wear**
**15** ~을 입다, 쓰다, 끼다, 신다, 착용하다

| wears | wore | worn |
|---|---|---|

Sena **wore** her new coat / proudly.
세나는 새 코트를 입었다 / 자랑스럽게

# Mini Test

A 빈칸에 알맞은 단어를 〈보기〉에서 찾아 쓰세요.

**1** That black suit really _____ you.

검정 양복이 너와 정말 어울린다.

**2** The sculptor _____ a wonderful statue out of marble.

조각가는 대리석으로 멋진 조각상을 조각했다.

**3** They _____ Bob on his Nobel Prize win.

그들은 밥의 노벨상 수상을 축하했다.

**4** They _____ the matter of free will.

그들은 자유 의지의 문제를 논의했다.

**5** Your behavior _____ who you are.

너의 행동은 네가 누구인지 정의한다.

**6** The judges _____ the key piece of evidence in this case.

판사는 이 사건에서 중요한 증거를 제외했다.

**7** The principal _____ the students about the new tests.

교장선생님은 새 시험에 대해 학생들에게 알렸다.

**8** The pipe _____ water.

그 관은 물이 샌다.

> 보기
>
> debated
> defines
> excluded
> becomes
> carved
> congratulated
> informed
> leaks

B 단어를 알맞게 배열하여 문장을 완성하세요.

**1** her head on the window.        She        leaned

_____

**2** married        My sister        a Chinese man.

_____

**3** The rider        her horse.        mounted

_____

**4** I        my pocket        searched        for money.

_____

**5** suggested        Mia        that I go see a doctor.

_____

**6** tore        People        the poster        off the wall.

_____

**7** her new coat        Sena        wore        proudly.

_____

C 다음 문장에서 동사를 찾아 동그라미하고, 해석을 써 보세요.

**1** Sena wore her new coat proudly.

_____

**2** People tore the posters off the wall.

_____

**3** I searched my pocket for money.

_____

**4** The rider mounted her horse.

_____

**5** Mia suggested that I go see a doctor.

_____

**6** My sister married a Chinese man.

_____

**7** She leaned her head on the window.

_____

**8** The pipe leaks water.

_____

**9** The principal informed the students about the new tests.

_____

**10** The judges excluded the key piece of evidence in this case.

_____

**11** Your behavior defines who you are.

_____

**12** They debated the matter of free will.

_____

**13** They congratulated Bob on his Nobel Prize win.

_____

**14** The sculptor carved a wonderful statue out of marble.

_____

**15** That black suit really becomes you.

_____

| | 3인칭/현재 | 과거 | 과거분사 |
|---|---|---|---|

**believe**

1  ~을 믿다

I **believe** he is honest.
나는 그가 정직하다는 것을 믿는다.

**board**

2  (배, 비행기, 차 등)에 타다

We **boarded** the plane / an hour before departure.
우리는 비행기에 탔다 / 출발 한 시간 전에

**cancel**

3  ~을 취소하다

I'd like to **cancel** my reservation.
나는 내 예약을 취소 하고 싶다.

**convict**

4  ~의 유죄를 입증하다

A jury **convicted** a woman of killing a neighbor.
배심원단은 여성에게 이웃을 살해한 혐의로 유죄를 선고했다.

**damage**

5  ~에 피해를 주다, 훼손하다

A fire **damaged** houses / in the city.
불이 집들을 훼손했다 / 도시의

**exchange**

6  ~을 교환하다, 바꾸다, 주고 받다

You can **exchange** an old cell phone / for a new one.
너는 오래된 휴대전화기를 바꿀 수 있다 / 새 것으로

**indicate**

7  ~을 나타내다, 표시하다, 가리키다,
보여 주다

She **indicated** a place / on a map.
그녀는 한 장소를 가리켰다 / 지도에서

## invent
**8** ~을 발명하다

Marchiony **invented** the ice cream cone / in the late 1800s.
마키오니가 아이스크림 콘을 발명했다 / 1800년대 후반에

## invest
**9** (자본, 돈 등)을 투자하다

Bill **invested** a lot of money / in stocks and shares.
빌은 많은 돈을 투자했다 / 채권과 주식에

## mention
**10** ~을 말하다, 언급하다

Did they **mention** my name?
그들이 내 이름을 말했니?

## read
**11** ~을 읽다

reads    read[red]    read[red]

I **read** all *Harry Potter* books / in English.
난 모든 〈해리포터〉 책들을 읽었다 / 영어로 된

## save
**12** ~을 구하다, (돈)을 저축하다

The boy **saved** all his money / to buy a bike.
그 소년은 모든 돈을 저축했다 / 자전거를 사기 위해

## swing
**13** ~을 흔들다, 휘두르다

swings    swung    swung

He **swung** the bat.
그는 야구방망이를 휘둘렀다.

## watch
**14** ~을 보다, 지켜보다

I **watched** the show.
나는 그 쇼를 봤다.

## work
**15** ~에게 일을 시키다; ~을 작동시키다

Employers can't **work** their employees / without payment.
고용주는 그들의 직원들에게 일을 시킬 수 없다 / 대가 없이

# Mini Test

**A** 빈칸에 알맞은 단어를 〈보기〉에서 찾아 쓰세요.

**1** I _____ he is honest.

나는 그가 정직하다는 것을 믿는다.

**2** We _____ the plane an hour before departure.

우리는 출발 한 시간 전에 비행기에 탔다.

**3** I'd like to _____ my reservation.

나는 예약을 취소 하고 싶다.

**4** A jury _____ a woman of killing a neighbor.

배심원단은 그녀에게 이웃을 살해한 혐의로 유죄를 선고했다.

**5** A fire _____ houses in the city.

불이 도시의 집들을 훼손했다.

**6** You can _____ an old cell phone for a new one.

너는 오래된 휴대전화기를 새 것으로 바꿀 수 있다.

**7** She _____ a place on a map.

그녀는 지도에서 한 장소를 가리켰다.

**8** Marchiony _____ the ice cream cone in the late 1800s.

마키오니가 1800년대 후반에 아이스크림 콘을 발명했다.

believe
indicated
invented
boarded
cancel
convicted
damaged
exchange

**B** 단어를 알맞게 배열하여 문장을 완성하세요.

**1** in stocks and shares.    invested    a lot of money    Bill

**2** mention    Did they    my name?

**3** read    all *Harry Potter* books    I    in English.

**4** saved    The boy    all his money    to buy a bike.

**5** He    the bat.    swung

**6** I    the show.    watched

**7** can't work    Employers    their employees    without payment.

112

C 다음 문장에서 동사를 찾아 동그라미하고, 해석을 써 보세요.

1 A jury convicted a woman of killing a neighbor.
_____

2 You can exchange an old cell phone for a new one.
_____

3 I'd like to cancel my reservation.
_____

4 I believe he is honest.
_____

5 A fire damaged a house in the city.
_____

6 We boarded a plane an hour before departure.
_____

7 She indicated a place on a map.
_____

8 I read all *Harry Potter* books in English.
_____

9 Marchiony invented the ice cream cone in the late 1800s.
_____

10 I watched the show.
_____

11 Bill invested a lot of money in stocks and shares.
_____

12 He swung the bat.
_____

13 The boy saved all his money to buy a bike.
_____

14 Employers can't work their employees without payment.
_____

15 Did they mention my name?
_____

MP3

| | 3인칭/현재 | 과거 | 과거분사 |
|---|---|---|---|

**blow**
1 ~을 불다, 소리를 내다

blows   blew   blown

She **blew** her whistle / to end the game.
그녀는 호루라기를 불었다 / 경기를 끝내려고

**book**
2 ~을 예약하다

I **booked** a table / at the Thai restaurant.
나는 테이블을 예약했다 / 태국 레스토랑에

**calculate**
3 ~을 계산하다

I'll **calculate** the cost of our trip / first.
나는 우리 여행 경비를 계산할 것이다 / 먼저

**detach**
4 ~을 잡아떼다, 떼어내다, 분리하다

**Detach** the bottom of the form.
양식의 하단을 떼어내라.

**examine**
5 ~을 조사하다, 심사하다, 시험을 실시
하다

The geologist **examined** a rock sample / from the cave.
지질학자가 암석 표본을 조사했다 / 동굴에서 나온

**improve**
6 ~을 개선하다, 더 좋게 하다

This workout will **improve** your health.
이 운동이 네 건강을 더 좋게 할 거다.

**interrupt**
7 ~을 방해하다, 차단하다, 가리다

My sister always **interrupts** me / while I'm trying to study.
우리 언니는 항상 나를 방해한다 / 내가 공부하려고 하는 동안

☐ **invade**
8 ~에 침입하다, 몰려들다

The enemy will **invade** our country.
적은 우리 나라를 침입할 것이다.

☐ **miss**
9 ~이 빗나가다, ~을 놓치다; 그리워하다

He **missed** the school bus.
그는 학교 버스를 놓쳤다.

☐ **respect**
10 ~를 존경하다

We should **respect** our elders.
우리는 어른들을 존경해야 한다.

☐ **reveal**
11 ~을 밝히다, 드러내다

The magician **revealed** his trick / to the audience.
그 마술사는 자신의 속임수를 밝혔다 / 관중에게

■ **swim**
12 ~을 헤엄치다

swims    swam    swum

They once **swam** the Straits of Korea.
그들은 한때 대한해협을 헤엄쳤다.

☐ **use**
13 ~을 쓰다, 이용하다

We all **use** social media / nowadays.
우리는 모두 소셜 미디어를 이용한다 / 요즘

☐ **want**
14 ~을 원하다, 바라다

I **want** a nice car.
나는 멋진 차를 원한다.

☐ **waste**
15 ~을 낭비하다

I've **wasted** too much time / worrying about little things.
나는 너무 많은 시간을 낭비했다 / 작은 것들에 고민하면서

A 빈칸에 알맞은 단어를 〈보기〉에서 찾아 쓰세요.

**1** She _____ her whistle to end the game.

그녀는 경기를 끝내려고 휘파람을 불었다.

**2** I _____ a table at the Thai restaurant.

나는 태국 레스토랑에 테이블을 예약했다.

**3** I'll _____ the cost of our trip first.

나는 먼저 우리 여행 경비를 계산할 것이다.

**4** _____ the bottom of the form.

양식의 하단을 떼어내라.

**5** The geologist _____ a rock sample from the cave.

지질학자가 동굴에서 나온 암석 표본을 조사했다.

**6** This workout will _____ your health.

이 운동이 네 건강을 더 좋게 할 거다.

**7** My sister always _____ me while I'm trying to study.

우리 언니는 내가 공부하려고 하는 동안 항상 나를 방해한다.

**8** The enemy will _____ our country.

적은 우리 나라를 침입할 것이다.

보기
blew
booked
interrupts
invade
calculate
Detach
examined
improve

B 단어를 알맞게 배열하여 문장을 완성하세요.

**1** He · the school bus. · missed

_____

**2** should respect · We · our elders.

_____

**3** The magician · his trick · revealed · to the audience.

_____

**4** They once · the Straits of Korea. · swam

_____

**5** use · We all · social media · nowadays.

_____

**6** I · a nice car. · want

_____

**7** wasted · I've · too much time · worrying about little things.

_____

C 다음 문장에서 동사를 찾아 동그라미하고, 해석을 써 보세요.

**1** I'll calculate the cost of our trip first.

_____

**2** We should respect our elders.

_____

**3** I want a nice car.

_____

**4** I booked a table at the Thai restaurant.

_____

**5** This workout will improve your health.

_____

**6** The geologist examined a rock sample from the cave.

_____

**7** The enemy will invade our country.

_____

**8** He missed the school bus.

_____

**9** My sister always interrupts me while I'm trying to study.

_____

**10** Detach the bottom of the form.

_____

**11** She blew her whistle to end the game.

_____

**12** They once swam the Straits of Korea.

_____

**13** I've wasted too much time worrying about little things.

_____

**14** We all use social media nowadays.

_____

**15** The magician revealed his trick to the audience.

_____

MP3

| | 3인칭/현재 | 과거 | 과거분사 |
|---|---|---|---|

**block**

1 ~을 막다, 봉쇄하다, 방해하다

We should **block** users / who behave badly online.
우리는 사용자들을 막아야 한다 / 온라인에서 나쁘게 행동하는

**bring** | brings | brought | brought

2 ~을 가져오다, 데려오다

You can **bring** your pets / to the party.
너는 반려동물을 데려올 수 있다 / 파티에

**bury**

3 (땅 속에) ~을 묻다

My grandma **buries** *kimchi* jars / every winter.
우리 할머니는 김장독을 묻는다 / 겨울마다

**cure**

4 ~을 낫게 하다, 치유하다

Can you **cure** my grandfather, Doctor?
우리 할아버지를 낫게 할 수 있나요, 의사 선생님?

**disappoint**

5 ~을 실망시키다, 좌절시키다

The results **disappointed** scientists.
그 결과는 과학자들을 실망시켰다.

**evaluate**

6 ~을 평가하다, 감정하다

The instructor will **evaluate** students' progress.
지도자가 학생들의 향상을 평가할 것이다.

**import**

7 ~을 수입하다

China **imports** coal / from North Korea.
중국은 석탄을 수입한다 / 북한으로부터

## insult
**8** ~을 모욕하다

We often **insult** someone / in anger.
우리는 종종 누군가를 모욕한다 / 화가 나서

## intend
**9** ~을 의도하다

She didn't **intend** to hurt Tasha.
그녀는 타샤를 상처 주려고 의도했던 것은 아니었다.

## mistake
**10** ~을 잘못 판단하다, 잘못 보다

mistakes　mistook　mistaken

I've **mistaken** you / for someone else.
저는 당신을 잘못 봤다 / 다른 사람으로

## rest
**11** ~을 쉬게 하다; ~에 기대다

He **rested** his head / on Tina's shoulder.
그는 자신의 머리를 기댔다 / 티나의 어깨에

## steal
**12** ~을 훔치다, 무단 사용하다

steals　stole　stolen

A thief **stole** the gold / from the bank.
도둑이 금을 훔쳤다 / 은행으로부터

## turn
**13** ~을 돌리다

She **turned** a key / to open the door.
그녀는 열쇠를 돌렸다 / 문을 열려고

## understand
**14** ~을 이해하다, 알아듣다

understands　understood　understood

He can **understand** French.
그는 불어를 이해할 수 있다.

## wake
**15** (잠에서) ~를 깨우다

She **woke** me up / before leaving.
그녀는 나를 깨웠다 / 떠나기 전에

**A** 빈칸에 알맞은 단어를 〈보기〉에서 찾아 쓰세요.

**1** We should _____ users who behave badly online.

우리는 온라인에서 나쁘게 행동하는 사용자들을 막아야 한다.

**2** You can _____ your pets to the party.

너는 파티에 반려동물을 데려올 수 있다.

**3** My grandma _____ *kimchi* jars every winter.

우리 할머니는 겨울마다 김장독을 묻는다.

**4** Can you _____ my grandfather, Doctor?

우리 할아버지를 낫게 할 수 있나요, 의사 선생님?

**5** The results _____ scientists.

그 결과는 과학자들을 실망시켰다.

**6** The instructor will _____ students' progress.

지도자가 학생들의 향상을 평가할 것이다.

**7** China _____ coal from North Korea.

중국은 북한으로부터 석탄을 수입한다.

**8** We often _____ someone in anger.

우리는 종종 화가 나서 누군가를 모욕한다.

보기

cure
disappointed
buries
evaluate
imports
block
bring
insult

**B** 단어를 알맞게 배열하여 문장을 완성하세요.

**1**　 didn't intend　　　　She　　　　to hurt Tasha.

_____

**2**　 mistaken　　　I've　　　　you　　　　for someone else.

_____

**3**　 rested　　　　He　　　　his head　　　　on her shoulder.

_____

**4**　 A thief　　　the gold　　　from the bank.　　　stole

_____

**5**　 She　　　to open the door.　　　turned　　　a key

_____

**6**　 can understand　　　French.　　　　He

_____

**7**　 woke　　　me up　　　She　　　before leaving.

_____

C 다음 문장에서 동사를 찾아 동그라미하고, 해석을 써 보세요.

1 He can understand French.

_____

2 She woke me up before leaving.

_____

3 A thief stole the gold from the bank.

_____

4 My grandma buries *kimchi* jars every winter.

_____

5 The instructor will evaluate students' progress.

_____

6 China imports coal from North Korea.

_____

7 The results disappointed scientists.

_____

8 I've mistaken you for someone else.

_____

9 He rested his head on Tina's shoulder.

_____

10 We often insult someone in anger.

_____

11 She didn't intend to hurt Tasha.

_____

12 She turned a key to open the door.

_____

13 You can bring your pets to the party.

_____

14 We should block users who behave badly online.

_____

15 Can you cure my grandfather, Doctor?

_____

MP3

| | 3인칭/현재 | 과거 | 과거분사 |
|---|---|---|---|

**blame**
1 ~를 비난하다

It's easy to **blame** others.
다른 사람을 비난하기는 쉽다.

**burn** — burns — burnt/burned — burnt/burned
2 ~을 태우다

I slightly **burnt** the toast / I made for breakfast.
나는 토스트를 약간 태웠다 / 아침식사로 만든

**call**
3 ~를 부르다; ~에게 전화하다

He **called** me / when I was in school.
그는 나에게 전화했다 / 내가 학교에 있을 때

**crowd**
4 (장소)를 가득 메우다, ~에 꽉 차다

Students **crowded** the lecture hall.
학생들은 강의당을 가득 메웠다.

**distinguish**
5 ~와 구별하다

Readers need to **distinguish** news from opinion.
독자는 의견과 뉴스를 구별할 필요가 있다.

**donate**
6 ~을 기부하다

A millionaire secretly **donated** lots of money / to charity.
백만장자가 몰래 많은 돈을 기부했다 / 자선 단체에

**estimate**
7 ~을 추정하다, 어림잡다, 평가하다

She **estimated** that the building would cost millions.
그녀는 그 빌딩이 백만 달러가 나갈 것이라 추정했다.

122

## imagine
**8** ~을 상상하다

He **imagined** himself / in Africa.
그는 자신을 상상했다 / 아프리카에 있는

## inspire
**9** ~을 불어넣다, ~에 영감을 주다

She **inspired** many girls / to reach for their goals.
그녀는 많은 소녀들에게 영감을 주었다 / 그들의 목표를 이루려는

## install
**10** ~을 설치하다, 설비하다

The repairman is going to **install** a new ceiling light.
수리공은 새 조명을 설치할 것이다.

## observe
**11** ~을 보다, 관찰하다

He **observed** people / in the street.
그는 사람들을 관찰했다 / 거리에서

## restore
**12** ~을 회복시키다, 복구하다

People tried to **restore** order / after the war.
사람들은 질서를 회복시키려고 노력했다 / 전쟁 후에

## return
**13** ~을 되돌려 놓다, 되돌려 주다

I'll **return** this book / to the library.
나는 이 책을 돌려줄 것이다 / 도서관에

## slide
**14** ~을 미끄러지게 하다, 미끄러뜨리다

slides    slid    slid

My aunt **slid** the pan / into the oven.
우리 이모가 팬을 미끄러뜨렸다 / 오븐 안으로

## wait
**15** ~을 기다리다

You should **wait** your turn.
너는 네 차례를 기다려야 한다.

# Mini Test

**A** 빈칸에 알맞은 단어를 〈보기〉에서 찾아 쓰세요.

**1** It's easy to _____ others.

다른 사람을 비난하기는 쉽다.

**2** I slightly _____ the toast I made for breakfast.

나는 아침식사로 만든 토스트를 약간 태웠다.

**3** He _____ me when I was in school.

내가 학교에 있을 때 그는 나에게 전화했다.

**4** Students _____ the lecture hall.

학생들은 강의당을 가득 메웠다.

**5** Readers need to _____ news from opinion.

독자는 의견과 뉴스를 구별할 필요가 있다.

**6** A millionaire secretly _____ lots of money to charity.

백만장자가 자선 단체에 몰래 많은 돈을 기부했다.

**7** She _____ that the building would cost millions.

그녀는 그 빌딩이 백만 달러가 나갈 것이라 추정했다.

**8** He _____ himself in Africa.

그는 자신이 아프리카에 있다고 상상했다.

> **보기**
> burnt
> called
> blame
> distinguish
> donated
> crowded
> estimated
> imagined

**B** 단어를 알맞게 배열하여 문장을 완성하세요.

**1**    She        many girls        inspired        to reach for their goals.

_____

**2**    is going to install        The repairman        a new ceiling light.

_____

**3**    He        people        observed        in the street.

_____

**4**    tried to restore        People        order        after the war.

_____

**5**    I'll        this book        return        to the library.

_____

**6**    My aunt        into the oven        slid the pan.

_____

**7**    You        your turn.        should wait

_____

C 다음 문장에서 동사를 찾아 동그라미하고, 해석을 써 보세요.

1 You should wait your turn.
_____

2 I'll return this book to the library.
_____

3 People tried to restore order after the war.
_____

4 My aunt slid the pan into the oven.
_____

5 He observed people in the street.
_____

6 The repairman is going to install a new ceiling light.
_____

7 He imagined himself in Africa.
_____

8 She estimated that the building would cost millions.
_____

9 She inspired many girls to reach for their goals.
_____

10 A millionaire secretly donated lots of money to charity.
_____

11 Readers need to distinguish news from opinion.
_____

12 It's easy to blame others.
_____

13 He called me when I was in school.
_____

14 Students crowded the lecture hall.
_____

15 I slightly burnt the toast I made for breakfast.
_____

MP3

|  | 3인칭/현재 | 과거 | 과거분사 |
|---|---|---|---|

### begin
1 ~을 하기 시작하다

begins   began   begun

When did you **begin** learning English?
언제 너는 영어를 배우기 시작했니?

### bully
2 ~를 괴롭히다

Five students **bullied** him / on the bus.
다섯 명의 학생이 그를 괴롭혔다 / 버스에서

### care
3 ~을 상관하다, 관심을 가지다

I don't **care** what you think.
나는 네가 무엇을 생각하는지 관심없다.

### change
4 ~을 바꾸다, 변화시키다

Pollution has **changed** the Earth's climate.
오염은 지구의 기후를 바꾸었다.

### cover
5 ~에 덮개를 씌우다, ~을 덮다

**Cover** the pot / with a lid.
냄비를 덮어라 / 뚜껑으로

### embarrass
6 ~를 당황하게 하다

His bad table manners **embarrassed** her.
그의 나쁜 식탁 예절이 그녀를 당황하게 했다.

### illustrate
7 (책 등에) 삽화를 넣다; ~을 설명하다

Mark **illustrated** how to use the software.
마크는 그 소프트웨어를 어떻게 사용하는지 설명했다.

## inhabit

**8** ~에 거주하다, 서식하다

Wild deer **inhabit** the forest.

야생 사슴이 그 숲에 산다.

## inject

**9** ~을 주사하다

The nurse **injected** the vaccine / into my arm.

그 간호사가 백신을 주사했다 / 내 팔에

## obtain

**10** ~을 얻다, 입수하다

You can **obtain** a driver's license / after passing the test.

너는 운전면허증을 얻을 수 있다 / 시험을 통과한 후

## resist

**11** ~에 저항하다

Kids can't **resist** chocolate.

아이들은 초콜릿에 참을 수 없다.

## ruin

**12** ~을 망치다, 파멸시키다

The heavy rain has **ruined** the plants.

폭우가 작물들을 망쳤다.

## slice

**13** ~을 얇게 썰다

**Slice** a tomato / for a sandwich.

토마토를 얇게 썰어라 / 샌드위치용으로

## try

**14** ~을 해 보다, 시도해 보다

She **tried** a new plan.

그녀는 새로운 계획을 시도해 봤다.

## visit

**15** ~을 방문하다, 머물다, 견학하다

I'll **visit** Busan / during summer vacation.

나는 부산을 방문할 것이다 / 여름 방학 동안에

**A** 빈칸에 알맞은 단어를 〈보기〉에서 찾아 쓰세요.

**1** When did you _____ learning English?

언제 너는 영어를 배우기 시작했니?

**2** Five students _____ him on the bus.

다섯 명의 학생이 버스에서 그를 괴롭혔다.

**3** I don't _____ what you think.

나는 네가 무엇을 생각하는지 관심없다.

**4** Pollution has _____ the Earth's climate.

오염은 지구의 기후를 바꾸었다.

**5** _____ the pot with a lid.

냄비를 뚜껑으로 덮어라.

**6** His bad table manners _____ her.

그의 나쁜 식탁 예절이 그녀를 당황하게 했다.

**7** Mark _____ how to use the software.

마크는 그 소프트웨어를 어떻게 사용하는지 설명했다.

**8** Wild deer _____ the forest.

야생 사슴이 그 숲에 산다.

보기

begin
Cover
illustrated
changed
bullied
embarrassed
care
inhabit

**B** 단어를 알맞게 배열하여 문장을 완성하세요.

**1**  injected    The nurse    the vaccine    into my arm.

_____

**2**  You    a driver's license    after passing the test.    can obtain

_____

**3**  Kids    chocolate.    can't resist

_____

**4**  has ruined    The heavy rain    the plants.

_____

**5**  Slice    for a sandwich.    a tomato

_____

**6**  tried    She    a new plan.

_____

**7**  visit    I'll    Busan    during summer vacation.

_____

C 다음 문장에서 동사를 찾아 동그라미하고, 해석을 써 보세요.

1 Wild deer inhabit the forest.
_____

2 Cover the pot with a lid.
_____

3 I don't care what you think.
_____

4 Mark illustrated how to use the software.
_____

5 Five students bullied him on the bus.
_____

6 His bad table manners embarrassed her.
_____

7 Pollution has changed the Earth's climate.
_____

8 When did you begin learning English?
_____

9 I'll visit Busan during summer vacation.
_____

10 You can obtain a driver's license after passing the test.
_____

11 The heavy rain has ruined the plants.
_____

12 She tried a new plan.
_____

13 Slice a tomato for a sandwich.
_____

14 Kids can't resist chocolate.
_____

15 The nurse injected the vaccine into my arm.
_____

MP3

| | 3인칭/현재 | 과거 | 과거분사 |
|---|---|---|---|

☐ **attribute**
1 ~의 탓으로 돌리다

He **attributed** his problems to bad luck.
그는 그의 잘못을 불운 탓으로 돌렸다.

■ **beat**    beats    beat    beaten
2 ~을 치다, 두드리다

She **beat** the drum / loudly.
그녀는 드럼을 쳤다 / 크게

☐ **brush**
3 ~을 솔질하다, 빗질하다

Jim **brushed** his hair / before going out.
짐은 자신의 머리카락을 빗질했다 / 나가기 전에

☐ **consider**
4 ~을 고려하다

We're **considering** getting a pet.
우리는 반려동물 갖는 것을 고려중이다.

☐ **count**
5 (총 수)를 세다, ~을 계산하다

He **counted** his change / out loud.
그는 자신의 잔돈을 세었다 / 소리 내어서

☐ **enhance**
6 ~을 높이다, 강하게 하다, 향상시키다

She **enhanced** her listening skills / via watching English dramas.
그녀는 자신의 듣기 실력을 향상시켰다 / 영어 드라마 보기를 통해

☐ **fascinate**
7 ~을 매료하다, 매혹하다

Jane **fascinated** me / when I saw her movie.
제인은 나를 매료시켰다 / 내가 그녀의 영화를 봤을 때

130

## □ imitate
**8** ~을 모방하다, 따라 하다

He was **imitating** the dancers / on the stage.
그는 댄서들을 모방하고 있었다 / 무대 위의

## □ impress
**9** ~를 감동시키다

The musical **impressed** the audience / with its songs and dances.
그 뮤지컬은 관중들을 감동시켰다 / 노래와 춤으로

## □ occupy
**10** ~을 차지하다, ~에 거주하다

The drama **occupied** my evenings / for a week.
그 드라마는 나의 저녁 시간을 차지했다 / 일주일 동안

## □ reserve
**11** ~을 예약하다

I'd like to **reserve** a table / for two.
나는 테이블을 예약하고 싶어요 / 두 사람을 위한

## ■ run
**12** ~를 달리다

runs    ran    run

I **ran** 100 meters / in twenty seconds.
나는 백 미터를 뛰었다 / 20초에

## □ settle
**13** ~을 해결하다, 끝내다, 정하다

We **settled** the problem.
우리는 그 문제를 해결했다.

## ■ sink
**14** ~을 침몰시키다, 파묻다

sinks    sank    sunk

He **sank** the boat / in the river.
그는 그 보트를 침몰시켰다 / 강에

## □ trust
**15** ~을 믿다, 신뢰하다

We **trust** him / to do right.
우리는 그를 믿는다 / 옳은 일을 하리라

**A** 빈칸에 알맞은 단어를 〈보기〉에서 찾아 쓰세요.

**1** He _____ his problems to bad luck.

그는 그의 잘못을 불운 탓으로 돌렸다.

**2** She _____ the drum loudly.

그녀는 크게 드럼을 쳤다.

**3** Jim _____ his hair before going out.

짐은 나가기 전에 자신의 머리카락을 빗질했다.

**4** We're _____ getting a pet.

우리는 반려동물을 가지는 것을 고려중이다.

**5** He _____ his change out loud.

그는 소리 내어서 자신의 잔돈을 세었다.

**6** She _____ her listening skills via watching English dramas.

그녀는 영어 드라마 보기를 통해 자신의 듣기 실력을 향상시켰다.

**7** Jane _____ me when I saw her movie.

내가 제인의 영화를 봤을 때 그녀는 나를 매료시켰다.

**8** He was _____ the dancers on the stage.

그는 무대 위의 댄서들을 모방하고 있었다.

> 보기
>
> fascinated
> imitating
> attributed
> beat
> brushed
> enhanced
> considering
> counted

**B** 단어를 알맞게 배열하여 문장을 완성하세요.

**1** impressed    The musical    the audience    with its songs and dances.

_____

**2** The drama    occupied    for a week.    my evenings

_____

**3** reserve    I'd like to    a table    for two.

_____

**4** I    100 meters    ran    in twenty seconds.

_____

**5** We    the problem.    settled

_____

**6** He    sank    in the river.    the boat

_____

**7** We    trust    to do right.    him

_____

C 다음 문장에서 동사를 찾아 동그라미하고, 해석을 써 보세요.

1 I'd like to reserve a table for two.
_____

2 She beat the drum loudly.
_____

3 He attributed his problems to bad luck.
_____

4 We're considering getting a pet.
_____

5 He counted his change out loud.
_____

6 She enhanced her listening skills via watching English dramas.
_____

7 The musical impressed the audience with its songs and dances.
_____

8 The drama occupied my evenings for a week.
_____

9 Jane fascinated me when I saw her movie.
_____

10 He sank the boat in the river.
_____

11 He was imitating the dancers on the stage.
_____

12 We trust him to do right.
_____

13 We settled the problem.
_____

14 Jim brushed his hair before going out.
_____

15 I ran 100 meters in twenty seconds.
_____

MP3

| | 3인칭/현재 | 과거 | 과거분사 |
|---|---|---|---|

### bear
1 ~을 참다, 견디다

bears    bore    borne

He couldn't **bear** the pain.
그는 고통을 참을 수 없었다.

### breathe
2 공기를 마시다

He **breathed** fresh air / while hiking.
그는 상쾌한 공기를 마셨다 / 하이킹하는 동안

### contact
3 ~에게 연락하다, 만나다

We'll **contact** you / by email.
우리는 당신에게 연락할 것이다 / 이메일로

### correct
4 ~을 바로잡다, 수정하다

Kane **corrected** himself / about the interview.
케인은 스스로 바로 잡았다 / 그 인터뷰에 대해

### engage
5 ~을 사로잡다, 고용하다, 약속하다

The doll didn't **engage** her interest / for long.
그 인형은 그녀의 관심을 끌지 못했다 / 오랫동안

### fasten
6 ~을 매다, 채우다

**Fasten** your seatbelt.
좌석벨트를 매세요.

### hire
7 ~를 고용하다, 세내다

Companies need to **hire** experts / to be successful.
회사들은 전문가를 고용할 필요가 있다 / 성공하려면

## hunt
**8** ~을 사냥하다, 샅샅이 찾다

They **hunted** a coyote / in winter.
그들은 코요테를 사냥했다 / 겨울에

## ignore
**9** ~를 무시하다

You mustn't **ignore** someone / if they talk to you.
너는 다른 사람을 무시해서는 안 된다 / 그들이 너에게 말할 때

## operate
**10** ~을 조작하다, 조종하다

Jina **operated** the microphone.
지나는 마이크를 조작했다.

## recognize
**11** ~을 알아보다

Don't you **recognize** me?
나 못 알아보겠어?

## represent
**12** ~을 대표하다, 대변하다, 변호하다

She **represented** her country / in the Olympics.
그녀는 자신의 조국을 대표했다 / 올림픽에서

## say
**13** ~을 말하다

| says | said | said |

I cannot **say** something that I don't believe.
난 내가 믿지 않는 어떤 것을 말할 수 없다.

## sing
**14** ~을 노래하다

| sings | sang | sung |

We **sang** the "Happy Birthday" song / at parties for my mom.
우리는 생일 축하 노래를 불렀다 / 파티에서 엄마를 위해

## treat
**15** ~을 다루다, 취급하다

You should **treat** this vase / with care.
너는 이 꽃병을 다뤄야만 한다 / 조심스럽게

A 빈칸에 알맞은 단어를 〈보기〉에서 찾아 쓰세요.

**1** He couldn't _____ the pain.

그는 고통을 참을 수 없었다.

**2** He _____ fresh air while hiking.

그는 하이킹하는 동안 상쾌한 공기를 마셨다.

**3** We'll _____ you by email.

우리는 이메일로 당신에게 연락할 것이다.

**4** Kane _____ himself about the interview.

케인은 스스로 그 인터뷰에 대해 바로 잡았다.

**5** The doll didn't _____ her interest for long.

오랫동안 그 인형은 그녀의 관심을 끌지 못했다.

**6** _____ your seatbelt.

좌석벨트를 매세요.

**7** Companies need to _____ experts to be successful.

회사들은 성공하려면 전문가를 고용할 필요가 있다.

**8** They _____ a coyote in winter.

그들은 겨울에 코요테를 사냥했다.

보기
engage
breathed
contact
bear
corrected
Fasten
hunted
hire

B 단어를 알맞게 배열하여 문장을 완성하세요.

**1** mustn't ignore　　　You　　　someone　　　if they talk to you.

_____

**2** 　　　Jina　　　the microphone.　　　operated

_____

**3** 　　　Don't you　　　me?　　　recognize

_____

**4** represented　　　She　　　her country　　　in the Olympics.

_____

**5** 　　　cannot say　　　I　　　something that I don't believe.

_____

**6** We　　　the "Happy Birthday" song　　　sang　　　at parties for my mom.

_____

**7** 　　　You　　　this vase　　　should treat　　　with care.

_____

C 다음 문장에서 동사를 찾아 동그라미하고, 해석을 써 보세요.

**1** He breathed fresh air while hiking.

_____

**2** He couldn't bear the pain.

_____

**3** Jina operated the microphone.

_____

**4** They hunted a coyote in winter.

_____

**5** You mustn't ignore someone if they talk to you.

_____

**6** Companies need to hire experts to be successful.

_____

**7** Kane corrected himself about the interview.

_____

**8** Fasten your seatbelt.

_____

**9** You should treat this vase with care.

_____

**10** I cannot say something that I don't believe.

_____

**11** We'll contact you by email.

_____

**12** Don't you recognize me?

_____

**13** She represented her country in the Olympics.

_____

**14** The doll didn't engage her interest for long.

_____

**15** We sang the "Happy Birthday" song at parties for my mom.

_____

| | 3인칭/현재 | 과거 | 과거분사 |
|---|---|---|---|

☐ **attend**

1 ~에 출석하다, 참석하다

Thousands **attended** this year's World Cup.
수천만이 올해 월드컵에 참석했다.

☐ **bother**

2 ~을 신경 쓰이게 하다, 괴롭히다

Traffic **bothered** the people / living near the ballpark.
교통체증이 사람들을 괴롭혔다 / 야구장 근처에 사는

☐ **continue**

3 ~을 계속하다

I'll **continue** to write letters / until he apologizes.
나는 편지를 계속 쓸 것이다 / 그가 사과할 때까지

☐ **copy**

4 ~을 베끼다, 복사하다

The teacher **copied** the worksheet / for his students.
선생님은 워크시트를 복사했다 / 학생들을 위해

☐ **encourage**

5 ~을 격려하다, ~에게 자신을 갖게 하다

My parents' support has **encouraged** me / greatly.
우리 부모님의 지원은 나를 격려했다 / 대단히

☐ **frustrate**

6 ~을 좌절시키다, 방해하다

My little sister sometimes **frustrates** my plans.
내 여동생은 가끔 내 계획을 방해한다.

■ **hang**

7 ~을 걸다, 매달다

hangs     hung     hung

I **hung** a picture of Noah / on the wall.
나는 노아의 사진을 걸었다 / 벽에

☐ **heal**

8 ~을 치유하다, 낫게 하다

The doctor **healed** Sean's broken leg.
의사는 션의 부러진 다리를 치료했다.

■ **hurt**

9 ~를 다치게 하다, 아프게 하다

hurts     hurt     hurt

The fire **hurt** two men / in the house.
불은 두 남자를 다치게 했다 / 집안에 있는

■ **overcome**

10 ~을 이겨내다, 극복하다

overcomes   overcame   overcome

The baseball pitcher **overcame** his injury.
야구 투수는 그의 부상을 극복했다.

☐ **receive**

11 ~을 받다

You should **receive** proper pay / for your work.
너는 제대로 급여를 받아야만 한다 / 네 일에 대한

☐ **reply**

12 ~에게 대답하다, ~을 답하다

He **replied** that he was busy.
그는 바빴다고 대답했다.

■ **see**

13 ~을 보다

sees     saw     seen

I **saw** some people / in the park.
나는 몇몇 사람들을 봤다 / 공원에서

☐ **shout**

14 ~을 외치다, 소리치다

She **shouted** that she found her son.
그녀는 자신의 아들을 찾았다고 소리쳤다.

☐ **transform**

15 (모습 등)을 달라지게 하다, 변형시키다

Mobile has **transformed** the retail industry.
휴대전화기가 소매업을 달라지게 했다.

A 빈칸에 알맞은 단어를 〈보기〉에서 찾아 쓰세요.

1 Thousands _____ this year's World Cup.

수천만이 올해 월드컵에 참석했다.

2 Traffic _____ the people living near the ballpark.

교통체증이 야구장 근처에 사는 사람들을 괴롭혔다.

3 I'll continue to _____ letters until he apologizes.

나는 그가 사과할 때까지 편지를 계속 쓸 것이다.

4 The teacher _____ the worksheet for his students.

선생님은 학생들을 위해 워크시트를 복사했다.

5 My parents' support has _____ me greatly.

우리 부모님의 지원은 나를 대단히 격려했다.

6 My little sister sometimes _____ my plans.

내 여동생은 가끔 내 계획을 방해한다.

7 I _____ a picture of Noah on the wall.

나는 벽에 노아의 사진을 걸었다.

8 The doctor _____ Sean's broken leg.

의사는 션의 부러진 다리를 치료했다.

| 보기 |
| --- |
| attended |
| frustrates |
| copied |
| healed |
| encouraged |
| bothered |
| hung |
| write |

B 단어를 알맞게 배열하여 문장을 완성하세요.

1 The fire     two men     hurt     in the house.

_____

2 overcame     The baseball pitcher     his injury.

_____

3 You     proper pay     should receive     for your work.

_____

4 He     that he was busy.     replied

_____

5 I     some people     in the park.     saw

_____

6 shouted     She     that she found her son.

_____

7 has transformed     Mobile     the retail industry.

_____

C 다음 문장에서 동사를 찾아 동그라미하고, 해석을 써 보세요.

1 I'll continue to write letters until he apologizes.
_____

2 The teacher copied the worksheet for his students.
_____

3 Thousands attended this year's World Cup.
_____

4 I hung a picture of Noah on the wall.
_____

5 Traffic bothered the people living near the ballpark.
_____

6 My little sister sometimes frustrates my plans.
_____

7 You should receive proper pay for your work.
_____

8 The baseball pitcher overcame his injury.
_____

9 He replied that he was busy.
_____

10 The doctor healed Sean's broken leg.
_____

11 She shouted that she found her son.
_____

12 The fire hurt two men in the house.
_____

13 I saw some people in the park.
_____

14 Mobile has transformed the retail industry.
_____

15 My parents' support has encouraged me greatly.
_____

| | 3인칭/현재 | 과거 | 과거분사 |
|---|---|---|---|

☐ **approve**

1 ~을 승인하다

The government will **approve** the new law / next week.
정부는 새 법을 승인할 것이다 / 다음 주에

☐ **borrow**

2 ~을 빌리다

Can I **borrow** your camera?
내가 네 카메라를 빌릴 수 있을까?

☐ **control**

3 ~을 지배하다, 관리하다

Pet owners must **control** their animals / at all times.
반려동물 주인들은 그들의 동물을 관리해야 한다 / 항상

☐ **convey**

4 ~을 전하다, 알리다

Nora's speech **conveyed** her confidence.
노라의 연설은 그녀의 자신감을 보여 주었다.

☐ **encounter**

5 (우연히) ~를 만나다, 마주치다

I **encountered** an old friend / on my way home.
나는 옛 친구를 만났다 / 집에 가는 길에

☐ **explore**

6 ~을 탐험하다, 조사하다

Janet has **explored** Africa.
자넷은 아프리카를 탐험했다.

☐ **fry**

7 ~을 기름에 굽다, 튀기다

He **fried** eggs and bacon / for lunch.
그는 계란과 베이컨을 구웠다 / 점심으로

### ☐ greet
**8** ~를 환영하다

The principal **greeted** the students / at the door.
교장은 학생들은 환영했다 / 문에서

### ☐ grip
**9** ~을 꽉 붙잡다, 세게 쥐다

**Grip** the rope / as hard as you can.
줄을 붙잡아라 / 네가 할 수 있는 한 단단히

### ■ hit
**10** ~을 때리다, 치다

| hits | hit | hit |
|---|---|---|

She **hit** the ball / too hard.
그녀는 볼을 쳤다 / 너무 세게

### ☐ permit
**11** ~을 허락하다

My mom didn't **permit** eating cookies / on the bed.
우리 엄마는 쿠키를 먹는 것을 허락하지 않았다 / 침대에서

### ☐ replace
**12** ~을 대신하다, 교체하다

The computer has **replaced** the typewriter.
컴퓨터는 타자기를 대신했다.

### ■ shoot
**13** ~을 쏘다, 발포하다

| shoots | shot | shot |
|---|---|---|

He **shot** the target / with his gun.
그는 목표물을 쏘았다 / 자신의 총으로

### ☐ start
**14** ~을 시작하다

The company will soon **start** selling drones.
그 회사는 곧 드론을 팔기 시작할 것이다.

### ☐ transfer
**15** 장소를 옮기다, 이동하다, 이전하다

You can **transfer** your homepage / to another account.
당신의 홈페이지를 옮길 수 있다 / 다른 계정으로

**A** 빈칸에 알맞은 단어를 〈보기〉에서 찾아 쓰세요.

**1** The government will _____ the new law next week.

정부는 다음 주에 새 법을 승인할 것이다.

**2** Can I _____ your camera?

내가 네 카메라를 빌릴 수 있을까?

**3** Pet owners must _____ their animals at all times.

반려동물 주인들은 항상 그들의 동물을 관리해야 한다.

**4** Nora's speech _____ her confidence.

노라의 연설은 그녀의 자신감을 보여 주었다.

**5** I _____ an old friend on my way home.

나는 집에 가는 길에 옛 친구를 만났다.

**6** Janet has _____ Africa.

자넷은 아프리카를 탐험했다.

**7** He _____ eggs and bacon for lunch.

그는 점심으로 계란과 베이컨을 구웠다.

**8** The principal _____ the students at the door.

교장은 문에서 학생들을 환영했다.

〈보기〉
control
approve
borrow
encountered
greeted
conveyed
explored
fried

**B** 단어를 알맞게 배열하여 문장을 완성하세요.

**1** the rope / Grip / as hard as you can.

**2** She / hit / too hard. / the ball

**3** didn't permit / My mom / eating cookies on the bed.

**4** has replaced / The computer / the typewriter.

**5** He / shot / with his gun. / the target

**6** will soon start / The company / selling drones.

**7** your homepage / You / can transfer / to another account.

C 다음 문장에서 동사를 찾아 동그라미하고, 해석을 써 보세요.

**1** Can I borrow your camera?

_____

**2** He shot the target with his gun.

_____

**3** I encountered an old friend on my way home.

_____

**4** Nora's speech conveyed her confidence.

_____

**5** She hit the ball too hard.

_____

**6** Pet owners must control their animals at all times.

_____

**7** He fried eggs and bacon for lunch.

_____

**8** The computer has replaced the typewriter.

_____

**9** Grip the rope as hard as you can.

_____

**10** Janet has explored Africa.

_____

**11** My mom didn't permit eating cookies on the bed.

_____

**12** The principal greeted the students at the door.

_____

**13** You can transfer your homepage to another account.

_____

**14** The government will approve the new law next week.

_____

**15** The company will soon start selling drones.

_____

| | 3인칭/현재 | 과거 | 과거분사 |
|---|---|---|---|

**1** ☐ **attract**
~을 끌어당기다, 매혹하다

A traditional cultural event can **attract** tourists.
전통적 문화 행사는 여행객들을 끌어당길 수 있다.

**2** ☐ **contribute**
~을 기부하다

The lawyer **contributed** money / to the fund.
그 변호사는 돈을 기부했다 / 기금에

**3** ■ **cut**     cuts     cut     cut
~을 베다, 상처 내다, 자르다

I **cut** my finger / on a coke can.
나는 내 손가락을 베었다 / 콜라 캔에

**4** ☐ **crack**
~을 금이 가게 하다

She **cracked** her mom's favorite china.
그녀는 엄마가 가장 좋아하는 자기 그릇에 금이 가게 했다.

**5** ☐ **emphasize**
~을 강조하다

The governor **emphasized** the importance of a vote.
주지사는 투표의 중요성을 강조했다.

**6** ■ **forgive**     forgives     forgave     forgiven
~을 용서하다

She **forgave** her little brother / who cut her books.
그녀는 동생을 용서했다 / 그녀의 책을 자른

**7** ☐ **gamble**
~을 도박으로 날리다

They **gambled** away their money.
그들은 자신들의 돈을 도박으로 날렸다.

## grab

**8** ~을 붙잡다, 움켜잡다, 가로채다

**Grab** the rope / to climb up.
줄을 잡아라 / 올라가게

## hide

**9** ~을 숨기다, 가리다

hides     hid     hidden

They **hid** the gifts / in the closet.
그들은 선물들을 숨겼다 / 옷장에

## hug

**10** ~을 껴안다, 끌어안다

A little girl **hugged** a doll / against her chest.
작은 소녀가 인형을 껴안았다 / 그녀의 가슴에

## pick

**11** ~을 뜯다, 고르다

I **picked** the biggest cookie / in the jar.
나는 가장 큰 쿠키를 집었다 / 병에서

## repeat

**12** ~을 반복하다, 되풀이하다, 전하다

She **repeated** the word / for emphasis.
그녀는 그 단어를 반복했다 / 강조하려고

## shake

**13** ~을 흔들다, 떨다

shakes     shook     shaken

The kid **shook** the bottle of soda.
그 아이는 탄산소다의 병을 흔들었다.

## sort

**14** ~을 분류하다, 구분하다

She has **sorted** her socks / by color.
그녀는 자신의 양말을 분류했다 / 색깔 별로

## trace

**15** ~의 자국을 따라가다, 추적하다

The hunter **traced** the rabbit's paw prints.
사냥꾼은 토끼의 발자국을 쫓았다.

# Mini Test

**A** 빈칸에 알맞은 단어를 〈보기〉에서 찾아 쓰세요.

**1** A traditional cultural event can _____ tourists.
전통적 문화 행사는 여행객들을 끌어당길 수 있다.

**2** The lawyer _____ money to the fund.
그 변호사는 기금에 돈을 기부했다.

**3** I _____ my finger on a coke can.
나는 콜라 캔에 내 손가락을 베었다.

**4** She _____ her mom's favorite china.
그녀는 엄마가 가장 좋아하는 자기 그릇에 금이 가게 했다.

**5** The governor _____ the importance of a vote.
주지사는 투표의 중요성을 강조했다.

**6** She _____ her little brother who cut her books.
그녀는 그녀의 책을 자른 동생을 용서했다.

**7** They _____ away their money.
그들은 자신들의 돈을 도박으로 날렸다.

**8** _____ the rope to climb up.
올라가게 줄을 잡아라.

보기: attract, emphasized, contributed, Grab, cut, forgave, cracked, gambled

**B** 단어를 알맞게 배열하여 문장을 완성하세요.

**1** hid / the gifts / They / in the closet.

**2** hugged / A little girl / a doll / against her chest.

**3** I / the biggest cookie / in the jar. / picked

**4** She / the word / repeated / for emphasis.

**5** The kid / the bottle of soda. / shook

**6** has sorted / She / her socks / by color.

**7** traced / The hunter / the rabbit's paw prints.

C 다음 문장에서 동사를 찾아 동그라미하고, 해석을 써 보세요.

1  I picked the biggest cookie in the jar.

 

2  She repeated the word for emphasis.

 

3  The kid shook the bottle of soda.

 

4  She has sorted her socks by color.

 

5  The hunter traced the rabbit's paw prints.

 

6  They hid the gifts in the closet.

 

7  A little girl hugged a doll against her chest.

 

8  The lawyer contributed money to the fund.

 

9  I cut my finger on a coke can.

 

10  She cracked her mom's favorite china.

 

11  The governor emphasized the importance of a vote.

 

12  She forgave her little brother who cut her books.

 

13  They gambled away their money.

 

14  Grab the rope to climb up.

 

15  A traditional cultural event can attract tourists.

 

MP3

| | 3인칭/현재 | 과거 | 과거분사 |
|---|---|---|---|

☐ **attack**

1  ~을 공격하다

Three terrorists **attacked** the church / last night.
세 명의 테러리스트들이 교회를 공격했다 / 지난 밤

☐ **acknowledge**

2  (~이 사실임)을 인정하다

We have to **acknowledge** the result / of the poll.
우리는 결과를 인정해야만 한다 / 투표의

☐ **bomb**

3  ~을 폭탄으로 공격하다

Terrorists **bombed** the city / in Latin America.
테러리스트들은 도시를 폭탄으로 공격했다 / 라틴아메리카의

☐ **contain**

4  ~이 들어 있다, 함유하다

Chocolate **contains** small amounts of caffeine.
초콜릿은 소량의 카페인이 들어 있다.

☐ **demand**

5  ~을 요구하다

He **demanded** payment of the debt.
그는 빚의 지불을 요구했다.

■ **drive**

6  ~을 몰다, 운전하다

drives    drove    driven

I'll **drive** a nice sports car / when I grow up.
나는 멋진 스포츠카를 몰 것이다 / 내가 자라면

■ **eat**

7  ~을 먹다

eats    ate    eaten

He **ate** a sandwich / for lunch.
그는 샌드위치를 먹었다 / 점심으로

☐ **fold**

**8** ~을 접다

Mom **folded** my sweaters / neatly into my suitcase.
엄마는 내 스웨터를 개켜 놓았다 / 깔끔하게 여행가방 안에

■ **forbid**

**9** ~을 금지하다

forbids    forbade    forbidden

Some countries still **forbid** alcoholic beverages.
몇몇 나라는 아직도 알코올 음료를 금지한다.

☐ **heat**

**10** ~을 뜨겁게 하다, 데우다

The stove **heated** the room.
난로가 방을 데웠다.

☐ **injure**

**11** ~을 다치게 하다, 상처를 입히다

June **injured** his leg / playing soccer.
준이는 다리를 다쳤다 / 축구를 하다가

☐ **predict**

**12** ~을 예측하다

I **predict** that today will be better.
나는 오늘이 더 나아질 거라고 예측한다.

☐ **repair**

**13** ~을 수리하다, 고치다

We **repaired** the roof of our house.
우리는 우리 집 지붕을 고쳤다.

☐ **scan**

**14** ~을 유심히 살피다

He **scanned** every student's face / for a while.
그는 모든 학생들의 얼굴을 유심히 살폈다 / 잠시 동안

☐ **tour**

**15** ~을 여행하다

They've **toured** South Africa / since last summer.
그들은 남아프리카를 여행했다 / 지난 여름 이래로

A 빈칸에 알맞은 단어를 〈보기〉에서 찾아 쓰세요.

**1** Three terrorists _____ the church last night.

지난 밤 세 명의 테러리스트들은 교회를 공격했다.

**2** We have to _____ the result of the poll.

우리는 투표의 결과를 인정해야만 한다.

**3** Terrorists _____ the city in Latin America.

테러리스트들이 라틴 아메리카의 도시를 폭탄으로 공격했다.

**4** Chocolate _____ small amounts of caffeine.

초콜릿은 소량의 카페인이 들어 있다.

**5** He _____ payment of the debt.

그는 빚의 지불을 요구했다.

**6** I'll _____ a nice sports car when I grow up.

나는 자라서 멋진 스포츠카를 몰 것이다.

**7** He _____ a sandwich for lunch.

그는 점심으로 샌드위치를 먹었다.

**8** Mom _____ my sweaters neatly into my suitcase.

엄마는 깔끔하게 여행가방 안에 내 스웨터를 개켜 놓았다.

| 보기 |
| --- |
| attacked |
| contains |
| acknowledge |
| demanded |
| folded |
| bombed |
| drive |
| ate |

B 단어를 알맞게 배열하여 문장을 완성하세요.

**1**     still forbid      Some countries      alcoholic beverages.

_____

**2**     The stove      the room.      heated

_____

**3**     June     playing soccer.     injured     his leg

_____

**4**     predict      I      that today will be better.

_____

**5**     We      the roof of our house.      repaired

_____

**6**     scanned     He     every student's face     for a while.

_____

**7**     They've     South Africa     toured     since last summer.

_____

**C** 다음 문장에서 동사를 찾아 동그라미하고, 해석을 써 보세요.

**1** Mom folded my sweaters neatly into my suitcase.

_____

**2** I predict that today will be better.

_____

**3** Three terrorists attacked the church last night.

_____

**4** Chocolate contains small amounts of caffeine.

_____

**5** The stove heated the room.

_____

**6** He demanded payment of the debt.

_____

**7** Some countries still forbid alcoholic beverages.

_____

**8** Terrorists bombed the city in Latin America.

_____

**9** I'll drive a nice sports car when I grow up.

_____

**10** He ate a sandwich for lunch.

_____

**11** He scanned every student's face for a while.

_____

**12** We have to acknowledge the result of the poll.

_____

**13** They've toured South Africa since last summer.

_____

**14** June injured his leg playing soccer.

_____

**15** We repaired the roof of our house.

_____

MP3

| | 3인칭/현재 | 과거 | 과거분사 |
|---|---|---|---|

☐ **appreciate**
1 ~에 감사하다

We **appreciate** your help.
우리는 당신의 도움에 감사한다.

☐ **assume**
2 ~을 추측하다

People **assumed** he was rich.
사람들은 그가 부자라고 추측했다.

☐ **boil**
3 ~이 끓다, ~을 끓이다

I'll **boil** water / for hot tea.
나는 물을 끓일 것이다 / 따뜻한 차를 위해

☐ **construct**
4 ~을 건설하다, 세우다

The company will **construct** a shopping center / in India.
그 회사는 쇼핑센터를 세울 것이다 / 인도에

☐ **cook**
5 ~을 요리하다

He was **cooking** fish / for dinner.
그는 생선을 요리하고 있었다 / 저녁식사로

☐ **design**
6 ~을 설계하다, 디자인하다

She is **designing** a new house / for her parents.
그녀는 새 집을 설계하고 있다 / 부모님을 위한

■ **drink**          drinks          drank          drunk
7 ~을 마시다

She **drinks** two liters of water / every day.
그녀는 2리터의 물을 마신다 / 매일

☐ **enjoy**

8  ~을 즐기다

I've **enjoyed** eating Thai food / for a long time.
나는 태국 음식 먹는 것을 즐겨왔다 / 오랫동안

☐ **fix**

9  ~을 수리하다, 고정하다

She **fixed** the saggy couch.
그녀는 푹 꺼진 소파를 고쳤다.

☐ **float**

10  ~을 뜨게 하다, 띄우다

The rising tide **floated** the small ship.
밀물이 작은 배를 띄웠다.

■ **hear**          hears          heard          heard

11  ~을 듣다, ~이 들리다

I **heard** the sound of crying.
나는 우는 소리를 들었다.

☐ **narrate**

12  ~을 말하다, 진술하다

The author **narrated** her story / to the audience.
그 작가는 그녀의 이야기를 말했다 / 관객에게

☐ **prefer**

13  ~을 선호하다, 더 좋아하다

I **prefer** ice cream / to chocolate.
나는 아이스크림을 더 좋아한다 / 초콜릿보다

☐ **remove**

14  ~을 제거하다, 없애다, 옮기다

Please **remove** the napkins / from the table.
냅킨을 치워 주세요 / 식탁에 있는

☐ **touch**

15  ~에 닿다, ~을 만지다

I **touched** the phone / to read the text messages.
나는 전화기를 만졌다 / 문자를 읽으려고

A 빈칸에 알맞은 단어를 〈보기〉에서 찾아 쓰세요.

**1** We _____ your help.

우리는 당신의 도움에 감사한다.

**2** People _____ he was rich.

사람들은 그가 부자라고 추측했다.

**3** I'll _____ water for hot tea.

나는 따뜻한 차를 위해 물을 끓일 것이다.

**4** The company will _____ a shopping center in India.

그 회사는 인도에 쇼핑센터를 세울 것이다.

**5** He was _____ fish for dinner.

그는 저녁식사로 생선을 요리하고 있었다.

**6** She is _____ a new house for her parents.

그녀는 부모님을 위한 새 집을 설계하고 있다.

**7** She _____ two liters of water every day.

매일 그녀는 2리터의 물을 마신다.

**8** I've _____ eating Thai food for a long time.

나는 오랫동안 태국 음식 먹는 것을 즐겨왔다.

보기

assumed
boil
appreciate
cooking
designing
enjoyed
construct
drinks

B 단어를 알맞게 배열하여 문장을 완성하세요.

**1** fixed　　　　She　　　　the saggy couch.

_____

**2** floated　　　　The rising tide　　　　the small ship.

_____

**3** I　　　　the sound of crying.　　　　heard

_____

**4** narrated　　　her story　　　The author　　　to the audience.

_____

**5** prefer　　　　I　　　　ice cream　　　　to chocolate.

_____

**6** Please remove　　　　from the table.　　　　the napkins

_____

**7** touched　　　I　　　the phone　　　to read the text messages.

_____

C 다음 문장에서 동사를 찾아 동그라미하고, 해석을 써 보세요.

**1** The company will construct a shopping center in India.

_____

**2** She is designing a new house for her parents.

_____

**3** I'll boil water for hot tea.

_____

**4** She fixed the saggy couch.

_____

**5** He was cooking fish for dinner.

_____

**6** We appreciate your help.

_____

**7** People assumed he was rich.

_____

**8** I heard the sound of crying.

_____

**9** She drinks two liters of water every day.

_____

**10** The rising tide floated the small ship.

_____

**11** I touched the phone to read the text messages.

_____

**12** Please remove the napkins from the table.

_____

**13** I prefer ice cream to chocolate.

_____

**14** I've enjoyed eating Thai food for a long time.

_____

**15** The author narrated her story to the audience.

_____

MP3

|  | 3인칭/현재 | 과거 | 과거분사 |
|---|---|---|---|

**☐ abandon**

1 ~을 버리다

How could you **abandon** our life-long friendship?

어떻게 너는 우리 일생의 우정을 버릴 수 있니?

**☐ address**

2 (~에게) 연설하다

The former president **addressed** the graduation ceremony.

전 대통령이 졸업식에서 연설을 했다.

**☐ bless**

3 ~에게 (신의) 축복을 빌다

Pastor Kim has **blessed** babies.

김 목사님이 아기들의 축복을 빌었다.

**☐ confirm**

4 ~을 확인해 주다

Duff has **confirmed** the rumor is true.

더프는 소문이 사실이라고 확인해 줬다.

**■ do**        does    did    done

5 (어떤 일)을 하다, 행하다

I'll **do** my duty / as the student president.

나는 내 의무를 할 것이다 / 학생 회장으로서

**■ draw**        draws    drew    drawn

6 ~을 끌다, 당기다

The donkey **drew** a cart / in a farm.

당나귀는 카트를 끌었다 / 농장에서

**☐ exceed**

7 ~을 넘다, 초과하다

Some drivers **exceed** the speed limit, / especially at night.

몇몇 운전자는 제한 속도를 넘는다 / 특히 밤에

☐ **excuse**

8 ~를 용서하다, 봐주다

Please **excuse** the interruption.
방해를 용서해 주세요.

☐ **guide**

9 ~에게 (길을) 안내하다

He **guided** us / across the square to the church.
그는 우리를 안내했다 / 광장을 지나 교회로

☐ **peel**

10 ~의 껍질을 벗기다

He can **peel** an orange / with one hand.
그는 오렌지 껍질을 벗길 수 있다 / 한 손으로

☐ **prepare**

11 ~을 준비하다

The fisherman **prepared** his net / for fishing.
그 어부는 그의 어망을 준비했다 / 물고기 잡이를 위해

☐ **relate**

12 ~을 관련시키다

Tim **related** his symptoms to the food he had eaten.
팀은 자신의 증상을 그가 먹은 음식과 관련시켰다.

☐ **release**

13 ~을 풀어 주다, 해방하다, 놓아주다, 풀다

The judge **released** the criminal / from prison.
판사는 그 범죄자를 석방시켰다 / 감옥에서

☐ **sail**

14 ~를 항해하다

Mark is going to **sail** the Pacific.
마크는 태평양을 항해할 것이다.

■ **throw**

15 ~을 던지다

throws　threw　thrown

Jina **threw** a ball / into the field.
지나는 공을 던졌다 / 들판으로

**A** 빈칸에 알맞은 단어를 〈보기〉에서 찾아 쓰세요.

**1** How could you _____ our life-long friendship?

어떻게 너는 우리 일생의 우정을 버릴 수 있니?

**2** The former president _____ the graduation ceremony.

전 대통령이 졸업식에서 연설을 했다.

**3** Pastor Kim has _____ babies.

김 목사님이 아기들의 축복을 빌었다.

**4** Duff has _____ the rumor is true.

더프는 소문이 사실이라고 확인해 줬다.

**5** I'll _____ my duty as the student president.

나는 학생 회장으로서 내 의무를 할 것이다.

**6** The donkey _____ a cart in a farm.

당나귀는 농장에서 카트를 끌었다.

**7** Some drivers _____ the speed limit, especially at night.

몇몇 운전자는 특히 밤에 제한 속도를 넘는다.

**8** Please _____ the interruption.

방해를 용서해 주세요.

보기

addressed

blessed

do

confirmed

abandon

drew

exceed

excuse

**B** 단어를 알맞게 배열하여 문장을 완성하세요.

**1** He     across the square     to the church.     guided us

_____

**2** He     an orange     can peel     with one hand.

_____

**3** prepared     The fisherman     his net     for fishing.

_____

**4** to the food he had eaten.     related     his symptoms     Tim

_____

**5** The judge     the criminal     from prison.     released

_____

**6** Mark     sail     is going to     the Pacific.

_____

**7** a ball     into the field.     threw     Jina

_____

C 다음 문장에서 동사를 찾아 동그라미하고, 해석을 써 보세요.

**1** Please excuse the interruption.

_____

**2** Some drivers exceed the speed limit, especially at night.

_____

**3** Duff has confirmed the rumor is true.

_____

**4** Pastor Kim has blessed babies.

_____

**5** He can peel an orange with one hand.

_____

**6** I'll do my duty as the student president.

_____

**7** Jina threw a ball into the field.

_____

**8** Mark is going to sail the Pacific.

_____

**9** The donkey drew a cart in a farm.

_____

**10** He guided us across the square to the church.

_____

**11** The fisherman prepared his net for fishing.

_____

**12** Tim related his symptoms to the food he had eaten.

_____

**13** The judge released the criminal from prison.

_____

**14** The former president addressed the graduation ceremony.

_____

**15** How could you abandon our life-long friendship?

_____

| | 3인칭/현재 | 과거 | 과거분사 |
|---|---|---|---|

☐ **admit**
1 (잘못이나 실수)를 인정하다

He never **admits** his mistakes.
그는 결코 자신의 실수들을 인정하지 않는다.

☐ **apply**
2 ~을 적용하다, 붙이다

**Apply** the lotion / evenly over the skin.
로션을 발라라 / 피부에 골고루

☐ **blend**
3 ~을 섞다

Elsa **blended** the flour / with the milk.
엘사는 밀가루를 섞었다 / 우유와

☐ **conduct**
4 ~을 처리하다, 지도하다

He **conducted** a test.
그는 시험을 지도했다.

☐ **doubt**
5 ~을 의심하다, 의혹을 갖다, 믿지 않다

Ann **doubted** Sue's honesty.
앤은 수의 정직함을 의심했다.

☐ **enter**
6 ~에 들어가다, 들어오다

My mom **entered** my room / without knocking.
우리 엄마는 내방에 들어왔다 / 문을 두드리지 않고

☐ **evolve**
7 ~을 (점점) 전개하다, 벌리다, 발전시키다

Plants **evolved** different ways / to survive.
식물들은 다른 방법들로 진화했다 / 살아남으려고

### ☐ exaggerate
**8** ~을 과장하다

She **exaggerates** any aches and pains.
그녀는 어떠한 통증과 아픔도 과장한다.

### ☐ face
**9** ~을 직면하다

Hilly **faced** her worst nightmare / – a room full of snakes!
힐리는 최악의 악몽을 마주했다 / 뱀으로 가득 찬 방!

### ☐ guess
**10** ~을 추측하다, 짐작하다

They **guessed** the result of the soccer match.
그들은 축구 경기의 결과를 추측했다.

### ☐ pollute
**11** ~을 오염시키다

Cars have **polluted** the environment.
자동차는 환경을 오염시켰다.

### ☐ preserve
**12** ~을 지키다, 보존하다, 유지하다

My grandfather has **preserved** an old way of life.
우리 할아버지는 옛 삶의 방식을 유지했다.

### ☐ reject
**13** ~을 거부하다, 불합격시키다

The villagers have **rejected** the development plan.
마을사람들은 그 계발 계획을 거절했다.

### ☐ rush
**14** ~을 서둘러 하게 하다, 급히 보내다

The firefighter **rushed** the sick / to a hospital.
소방관이 서둘러 환자들을 운송했다 / 병원으로

### ☐ tie
**15** ~을 묶다, 매다

The little boy **tied** his shoelaces / by himself.
어린 소년이 자신의 신발끈을 묶었다 / 혼자

**A** 빈칸에 알맞은 단어를 〈보기〉에서 찾아 쓰세요.

**1** He never _____ his mistakes.

그는 결코 자신의 실수들을 인정하지 않는다.

**2** _____ the lotion evenly over the skin.

피부에 골고루 로션을 발라라.

**3** Elsa _____ the flour with the milk.

엘사는 우유와 밀가루를 섞었다.

**4** He _____ a test.

그는 시험을 지도했다.

**5** Ann _____ Sue's honesty.

앤은 수의 정직함을 의심했다.

| 보기 |
| --- |
| conducted |
| doubted |
| admits |
| Apply |
| entered |
| evolved |
| blended |
| exaggerates |

**6** My mom _____ my room without knocking.

우리 엄마는 문을 두드리지 않고 내방에 들어왔다.

**7** Plants _____ different ways to survive.

식물들은 살아남으려고 다른 방법들로 진화했다.

**8** She _____ any aches and pains.

그녀는 어떠한 통증과 아픔도 과장한다.

**B** 단어를 알맞게 배열하여 문장을 완성하세요.

**1**  Hilly    – a room full of snakes!    faced    her worst nightmare

_____

**2**  They    the result    of the soccer match.    guessed

_____

**3**  Cars    the environment.    have polluted

_____

**4**  My grandfather    an old way of life.    has preserved

_____

**5**  The villagers    the development plan.    have rejected

_____

**6**  The firefighter    the sick    to a hospital.    rushed

_____

**7**  The little boy    his shoelaces    by himself.    tied

_____

C 다음 문장에서 동사를 찾아 동그라미하고, 해석을 써 보세요.

1 She exaggerates any aches and pains.
_____

2 Cars have polluted the environment.
_____

3 Ann doubted Sue's honesty.
_____

4 Plants evolved different ways to survive.
_____

5 Apply the lotion evenly over the skin.
_____

6 Elsa blended the flour with the milk.
_____

7 My grandfather has preserved an old way of life.
_____

8 He conducted a test.
_____

9 The firefighter rushed the sick to a hospital.
_____

10 The little boy tied his shoelaces by himself.
_____

11 They guessed the result of the soccer match.
_____

12 He never admits his mistakes.
_____

13 My mom entered my room without knocking.
_____

14 The villagers have rejected the development plan.
_____

15 Hilly faced her worst nightmare – a room full of snakes!
_____

| | 3인칭/현재 | 과거 | 과거분사 |
|---|---|---|---|

□ **arrest**
1 ~를 체포하다

Police **arrested** the teenage robber / on Monday.
경찰은 십대 강도를 붙잡았다 / 월요일에

■ **bite** — bites | bit | bitten
2 ~을 물다, 물어 뜯다

A shark **bit** a man / who was surfing in the water.
상어가 남자를 물었다 / 물에서 서핑하고 있던

■ **choose** — chooses | chose | chosen
3 ~을 고르다, 선택하다

She **chose** the red dress / for the party.
그녀는 빨간색 원피스를 선택했다 / 파티를 위해

□ **conclude**
4 ~을 끝내다

They **concluded** their argument / by shaking hands.
그들은 언쟁을 끝냈다 / 악수를 함으로써

□ **enclose**
5 ~을 (담, 벽 등으로) 둘러싸다, 에워싸다

Mona **enclosed** her garden / with flowers.
모나는 자신의 정원을 둘러쌌다 / 꽃으로

□ **endure**
6 ~을 참다, 견디다

I cannot **endure** your insults any longer.
나는 너의 모욕을 견딜 수 없다 / 더 이상

■ **feel** — feels | felt | felt
7 ~을 느끼다, 감지하다

He **felt** a sudden pain.
그는 갑작스런 통증을 느꼈다.

## grow

**8**　~을 키우다

grows　grew　grown

I've **grown** lots of vegetables / in my balcony garden.
나는 많은 채소를 키웠다 / 내 베란다 정원에

## need

**9**　~이 필요하다

Plants **need** water / in order to survive.
식물은 물이 필요하다 / 살아남기 위해

## offer

**10**　~을 제안하다

We **offered** an idea / to the company.
우리는 아이디어를 제안했다 / 그 회사에

## press

**11**　~을 누르다, 압축하다

I **pressed** the elevator button.
나는 엘리베이터 버튼을 눌렀다.

## refuse

**12**　~을 거절하다, 거부하다

He **refused** the money / from his boss.
그는 그 돈을 거절했다 / 자신의 상관으로부터

## rob

**13**　~에게서 빼앗다

The man **robbed** me / of my purse.
그 남자는 나에게서 지갑을 빼앗았다.

## shave

**14**　~를 면도하다

I **shaved** my own head.
나는 내 머리를 면도했다.

## teach

**15**　~을[~에게] 가르치다

teaches　taught　taught

She **taught** English / to me.
그녀는 영어를 가르쳤다 / 나에게

# Mini Test

**A** 빈칸에 알맞은 단어를 〈보기〉에서 찾아 쓰세요.

**1** Police _____ the teenage robber on Monday.

경찰은 월요일에 십대 강도를 붙잡았다.

**2** A shark _____ a man who was surfing in the water.

상어가 물에서 서핑하고 있던 남자를 물었다.

**3** She _____ the red dress for the party.

그녀는 파티를 위해 빨간색 원피스를 선택했다.

**4** They _____ their argument by shaking hands.

그들은 악수함으로써 언쟁을 끝냈다.

**5** Mona _____ her garden with flowers.

모나는 꽃으로 자신의 정원을 둘러쌌다.

**6** I cannot _____ your insults any longer.

나는 더 이상 너의 모욕을 견딜 수 없다.

**7** He _____ a sudden pain.

그는 갑작스런 통증을 느꼈다.

**8** I've _____ lots of vegetables in my balcony garden.

나는 내 베란다 정원에 많은 채소를 키웠다.

보기
bit
concluded
chose
arrested
enclosed
felt
endure
grown

**B** 단어를 알맞게 배열하여 문장을 완성하세요.

**1** need　　Plants　　water in order to survive.

_____

**2** offered　　We　　an idea to the company.

_____

**3** I　　the elevator button.　　pressed

_____

**4** He　　refused　　from his boss.　　the money

_____

**5** robbed　　The man　　me of my purse.

_____

**6** I　　my own head.　　shaved

_____

**7** taught　　She　　English　　to me.

_____

168

C 다음 문장에서 동사를 찾아 동그라미하고, 해석을 써 보세요.

**1** They concluded their argument by shaking hands.

_____

**2** I cannot endure your insults any longer.

_____

**3** She chose the red dress for the party.

_____

**4** Police arrested the teenage robber on Monday.

_____

**5** Mona enclosed her garden with flowers.

_____

**6** A shark bit a man who was surfing in the water.

_____

**7** I pressed the elevator button.

_____

**8** I've grown lots of vegetables in my balcony garden.

_____

**9** He felt a sudden pain.

_____

**10** She taught English to me.

_____

**11** Plants need water in order to survive.

_____

**12** He refused the money from his boss.

_____

**13** I shaved my own head.

_____

**14** We offered an idea to the company.

_____

**15** The man robbed me of my purse.

_____

MP3

| | 3인칭/현재 | 과거 | 과거분사 |
|---|---|---|---|

**bind**
1 ~을 묶다

binds | bound | bound

He **bound** the dog / to a chair.
그는 그 개를 묶었다 / 의자에

**divide**
2 ~을 나누다, 쪼개다

Mrs. Cho **divided** the class / into two teams.
조 선생님은 반을 나누었다 / 두 개의 팀으로

**edit**
3 (책)을 편집하다

Steve has **edited** English books / for beginners.
스티브는 영어책을 편집했다 / 초보자용

**elect**
4 ~을 선출하다, 뽑다

We **elect** politicians / to represent us.
우리는 정치인을 뽑는다 / 우리를 대변할

**establish**
5 ~을 설립하다

China **established** the largest solar power station.
중국은 가장 큰 태양광 발전소를 설립했다.

**figure**
6 ~을 계산하다, 판단하다, 모양을 이루다

He **figured** his total grade point average.
그는 자신의 성적의 평점을 계산했다.

**grant**
7 ~을 승인하다, 허락하다

Cornell University **granted** our request / to visit.
코넬 대학은 우리의 요청을 승인했다 / 방문하려는

**mind**

**8** ~을 언짢아하다, 마음을 쓰다

Do you **mind** opening the window?
창문을 여는 게 신경 쓰이니? (창문을 열어도 될까?)

**move**

**9** ~을 옮기다, 이동하다

We **moved** the furniture / in our living room.
우리는 가구를 옮겼다 / 우리 거실에 있는

**prevent**

**10** ~을 예방하다, 방지하다, 막다

I **prevent** my brother / from touching my phone.
나는 내 동생을 막았다 / 내 휴대전화기를 만지는 것으로부터

**reform**

**11** ~을 개선하다, 교화시키다

The fruit company **reformed** its storage system.
그 과일 회사는 저장 시스템을 개선했다.

**ride**            rides      rode      ridden

**12** ~을 타다, 말을 타고 가다

They will **ride** city buses / for free throughout the day.
그들은 시내 버스를 탈 것이다 / 공짜로 낮 동안

**shame**

**13** ~을 창피하게 하다

Kevin's rude behavior **shamed** his family.
케빈의 무례한 행동은 자신의 가족을 창피하게 했다.

**switch**

**14** ~을 바꾸다, 교환하다

Mia **switched** places / with Jamie in the line.
미아는 자리를 바꿨다 / 제이미와 줄 서 있는

**yell**

**15** ~을[~에게] 소리치다

The waiter **yelled** an order / to the kitchen.
웨이터는 주문을 소리쳤다 / 주방에

## Mini Test

A 빈칸에 알맞은 단어를 〈보기〉에서 찾아 쓰세요.

1 He _____ the dog to a chair.
그는 그 개를 의자에 묶었다.

2 Mrs. Cho _____ the class into two teams.
조 선생님은 반을 두 개의 팀으로 나누었다.

3 Steve has _____ English books for beginners.
스티브는 초보자용 영어책을 편집했다.

4 We _____ politicians to represent us.
우리는 우리를 대변할 정치인을 뽑는다.

5 China _____ the largest solar power station.
중국은 가장 큰 태양광 발전소를 설립했다.

6 He _____ his total grade point average.
그는 자신의 성적의 평점을 계산했다.

7 Cornell University _____ our request to visit.
코넬 대학은 우리의 방문 요청을 승인했다.

8 Do you _____ opening the window?
창문을 여는 게 신경 쓰이니? (창문을 열어도 될까?)

보기
divided
bound
edited
established
elect
mind
figured
granted

B 단어를 알맞게 배열하여 문장을 완성하세요.

1 the furniture   We moved   in our living room.
_____

2 I prevent   from touching my phone.   my brother
_____

3 reformed   The fruit company   its storage system.
_____

4 city buses   They will   ride   for free throughout the day.
_____

5 shamed   Kevin's rude behavior   his family.
_____

6 Mia switched   with Jamie in the line.   places
_____

7 The waiter   to the kitchen.   yelled   an order
_____

172

C 다음 문장에서 동사를 찾아 동그라미하고, 해석을 써 보세요.

1 We moved the furniture in our living room.

_____

2 I prevent my brother from touching my phone.

_____

3 The fruit company reformed its storage system.

_____

4 They will ride city buses for free throughout the day.

_____

5 Kevin's rude behavior shamed his family.

_____

6 Mia switched places with Jamie in the line.

_____

7 The waiter yelled an order to the kitchen.

_____

8 Do you mind opening the window?

_____

9 He bound the dog to a chair.

_____

10 Mrs. Cho divided the class into two teams.

_____

11 Steve has edited English books for beginners.

_____

12 We elect politicians to represent us.

_____

13 China established the largest solar power station.

_____

14 He figured his total grade point average.

_____

15 Cornell University granted our request to visit.

_____

MP3

| | 3인칭/현재 | 과거 | 과거분사 |
|---|---|---|---|

☐ **anticipate**
1 ~을 예상하다

AI can **anticipate** human behavior.
인공지능은 인간의 행동을 예상할 수 있다.

■ **bend**
2 ~을 구부리다

bends    bent    bent

She **bent** the wire / by hand.
그녀는 철사를 구부렸다 / 손으로

☐ **charge**
3 ~을 청구하다

The shop **charges** too much money / for its goods.
그 상점은 너무 많은 돈을 청구한다 / 물건 값으로

☐ **divorce**
4 ~와 이혼하다, 이혼시키다

Noa **divorced** his wife / after two years of marriage.
노아는 그의 부인과 이혼했다 / 결혼 2년 후

☐ **drag**
5 (무거운 것을) 끌다, 끌어 당기다

They **dragged** the wardrobe / away from the wall.
그들은 그 옷장을 끌어 당겼다 / 벽에서 멀리

☐ **follow**
6 ~을 따라가다, 뒤따르다, 이해하다

The officer was **following** a man / who stole a wallet.
경찰은 한 남자를 따라가고 있었다 / 지갑을 훔친

☐ **gain**
7 (원하던 것)을 얻다

I **gained** the first prize / for the first time.
나는 일등상을 받았다 / 처음으로

**include**

8   ~을 포함하다, 함유하다

The price **includes** all of your food / during the trip.
그 가격은 당신의 모든 식사비를 포함한다 / 여행 동안

**mean**     means     meant     meant

9   ~을 의미하다, 뜻하다

A red circle with a line **means** you cannot enter.
선이 있는 빨간 원은 네가 들어갈 수 없다는 것을 의미한다.

**promote**

10   ~을 촉진하다, 장려하다

The UN **promotes** world peace.
유엔은 세계 평화를 장려한다.

**reduce**

11   ~을 줄이다, 축소하다

We should **reduce** our food waste.
우리는 음식 쓰레기를 줄여야만 한다.

**relieve**

12   ~을 없애주다, 완화하다

The pill will **relieve** your headache.
그 알약은 네 두통을 없애 줄 거다.

**remind**

13   ~에게 생각나게 하다

He **reminds** me / of my old friend.
그는 나에게 생각나게 한다 / 옛 친구를

**see**     sees     saw     seen

14   ~을 보다

I **saw** my teacher / in the park.
나는 우리 선생님을 봤다 / 공원에서

**suppose**

15   ~라고 생각하다, 추측하다

What do you **suppose** he will do?
너는 그가 무엇을 할 것이라고 생각하니?

## Mini Test

### A 빈칸에 알맞은 단어를 〈보기〉에서 찾아 쓰세요.

**1** AI can _____ human behavior.

인공지능은 인간의 행동을 예상할 수 있다.

**2** She _____ the wire by hand.

그녀는 철사를 손으로 구부렸다.

**3** The shop _____ too much money for its goods.

그 상점은 너무 많은 돈을 물건 값으로 청구한다.

**4** Noa _____ his wife after two years of marriage.

노아는 그의 부인과 결혼 2년 후에 이혼했다.

**5** They _____ the wardrobe away from the wall.

그들은 그 옷장을 벽에서 멀리 끌어 당겼다.

**6** The officer was _____ a man who stole a wallet.

경찰은 지갑을 훔친 한 남자를 따라가고 있었다.

**7** I _____ the first prize for the first time.

나는 처음으로 일등상을 받았다.

**8** The price _____ all of your food during the trip.

그 가격은 여행 동안 당신의 모든 식사비를 포함한다.

보기

bent
charges
anticipate
divorced
dragged
following
includes
gained

### B 단어를 알맞게 배열하여 문장을 완성하세요.

**1** means | A red circle with a line | you cannot enter.

_____

**2** promotes | The UN | world peace.

_____

**3** We should | our food waste. | reduce

_____

**4** The pill | your headache. | will relieve

_____

**5** reminds | He | me | of my old friend.

_____

**6** I | my teacher | saw | in the park.

_____

**7** do you suppose | What | he will do?

_____

176

C 다음 문장에서 동사를 찾아 동그라미하고, 해석을 써 보세요.

1 A red circle with a line means you cannot enter.

_____

2 The UN promotes world peace.

_____

3 We should reduce our food waste.

_____

4 He reminds me of my old friend.

_____

5 The pill will relieve your headache.

_____

6 I saw my teacher in the park.

_____

7 What do you suppose he will do?

_____

8 She bent the wire by hand.

_____

9 The shop charges too much money for its goods.

_____

10 Noa divorced his wife after two years of marriage.

_____

11 They dragged the wardrobe away from the wall.

_____

12 The officer was following a man who stole a wallet.

_____

13 I gained the first prize for the first time.

_____

14 The price includes all of your food during the trip.

_____

15 AI can anticipate human behavior.

_____

| | 3인칭/현재 | 과거 | 과거분사 |
|---|---|---|---|

☐ **appoint**

1 ~를 임명하다

They **appointed** him / as the head chef.
그들은 그를 임명했다 / 수석 요리사로

☐ **ban**

2 ~을 금하다

Forestry officials **banned** camp fires.
산림 관리 사무소는 캠프 파이어를 금지했다.

■ **catch**      catches    caught    caught

3 ~을 잡다

He **caught** a fish / with his bare hands.
그는 물고기를 잡았다 / 자신의 맨 손으로

☐ **discuss**

4 ~을 논의하다, 의논하다

They **discussed** the future of the school union.
그들은 학교 연합의 미래를 논의했다.

☐ **distribute**

5 ~을 나누어 주다, 분배하다, 배부하다

Mother Theresa **distributed** everything she had / to the poor.
테레사 수녀는 그녀가 가진 모든 것을 나누어 줬다 / 가난한 자들에게

☐ **disturb**

6 ~을 방해하다

Don't **disturb** me / while I am studying.
나를 방해하지 마라 / 내가 공부하고 있는 동안에

☐ **escape**

7 ~을 피하다, 면하다

We cannot **escape** punishment.
우리는 처벌을 피할 수 없다.

☐ **force**
8  ~에게 강요하다, 시키다

You can't **force** them / to stop.
너는 그들에게 강요할 수 없다 / 멈추라고

■ **forget**  forgets  forgot  forgotten
9  ~을 잊다, 기억 못 하다

My grandmother often **forgets** people's names.
우리 할머니는 종종 사람들의 이름을 잊는다.

■ **make**  makes  made  made
10  ~을 만들다

Ed **made** some cookies / for his mom.
에드는 쿠키를 만들었다 / 자신의 엄마를 위해

■ **prove**  proves  proved  proved/proven
11  ~을 입증하다

The facts **proved** the man's innocence.
그 사실은 그 남자의 무죄를 입증했다.

☐ **qualify**
12  ~에게 자격을 주다

Passing this test **qualifies** you / to join our club.
이 시험에 합격하면 너희에게 자격을 준다 / 우리 동아리에 함께 할

■ **quit**  quits  quit/quitted  quit/quitted
13  ~을 그만 두다, 떠나다

She **quitted** her job / too easily.
그녀는 일을 그만 뒀다 / 너무 쉽게

☐ **recover**
14  ~을 되찾다, 회복하다

You cannot **recover** deleted files / on your smart phone.
너는 삭제한 파일을 복구할 수 없다 / 네 스마트폰의

☐ **succeed**
15  ~의 뒤를 잇다

He **succeeded** his father / as a manager of the firm.
그는 그의 아버지의 뒤를 이었다 / 회사의 매니저로

**A** 빈칸에 알맞은 단어를 〈보기〉에서 찾아 쓰세요.

**1** They _____ him as the head chef.

그들은 그를 수석 요리사로 임명했다.

**2** Forestry officials _____ camp fires.

산림 관리 사무소는 캠프 파이어를 금지했다.

**3** He _____ a fish with his bare hands.

그는 맨 손으로 물고기를 잡았다.

**4** They _____ the future of the school union.

그들은 학교 연합의 미래를 논의했다.

**5** Mother Theresa _____ everything she had to the poor.

테레사 수녀는 그녀가 가진 모든 것을 가난한 자들에게 나누어 줬다.

**6** Don't _____ me while I am studying.

내가 공부하고 있는 동안에 나를 방해하지 마라.

**7** We cannot _____ punishment.

우리는 처벌을 피할 수 없다.

**8** You can't _____ them to stop.

너는 그들에게 멈추라고 강요할 수 없다.

보기
- banned
- caught
- appointed
- distributed
- escape
- disturb
- force
- discussed

**B** 단어를 알맞게 배열하여 문장을 완성하세요.

**1** often forgets    My grandmother    people's names.

_____

**2** some cookies    made    Ed    for his mom.

_____

**3** proved    the man's innocence.    The facts

_____

**4** qualifies    Passing this test    to join our club.    you

_____

**5** her job    She    too easily.    quitted

_____

**6** on your smart phone.    deleted files    You    cannot recover

_____

**7** his father    He    succeeded    as a manager of the firm.

_____

C 다음 문장에서 동사를 찾아 동그라미하고, 해석을 써 보세요.

**1** She quitted her job too easily.

_____

**2** Passing this test qualifies you to join our club.

_____

**3** He succeeded his father as a manager of the firm.

_____

**4** Ed made some cookies for his mom.

_____

**5** Forestry officials banned camp fires.

_____

**6** They appointed him as the head chef.

_____

**7** He caught a fish with his bare hands.

_____

**8** The facts proved the man's innocence.

_____

**9** We cannot escape punishment.

_____

**10** My grandmother often forgets people's names.

_____

**11** They discussed the future of the school union.

_____

**12** You cannot recover deleted files on your smart phone.

_____

**13** Mother Theresa distributed everything she had to the poor.

_____

**14** You can't force them to stop.

_____

**15** Don't disturb me while I am studying.

_____

MP3

| | 3인칭/현재 | 과거 | 과거분사 |
|---|---|---|---|

**1** ☐ **award**
~을 수여하다, 판정을 내리다

They **awarded** first prize / to Laura.
그들은 일등상을 수여했다 / 로라에게

**2** ■ **cast**
~을 던지다; (눈길)을 주다

| | casts | cast | cast |
|---|---|---|---|

The fisherman **cast** the fish / back into the river.
어부는 그 물고기를 던졌다 / 다시 강으로

**3** ☐ **detect**
~을 알아내다, 발견하다, 찾아내다

Robots can **detect** illness / in its early stage.
로봇이 병을 발견할 수 있다 / 초기 단계에서

**4** ☐ **discover**
~을 발견하다, 찾아내다

Alexander Fleming **discovered** penicillin.
알렉산더 플레밍은 페니실린을 발견했다.

**5** ☐ **disgust**
~을 역겹게 하다

The smell **disgusts** me.
그 냄새가 나를 역겹게 한다.

**6** ☐ **dismiss**
~을 떠나게 하다, 보내다, 해고하다

The company will **dismiss** five percent of its employees.
그 회사는 5 퍼센트의 직원을 해고할 것이다.

**7** ■ **fly**
(새, 연 등)을 날리다, 놓아주다

| | flies | flew | flown |
|---|---|---|---|

He **flew** his kite / in the park.
그는 연을 날렸다 / 공원에서

## form
**8** (형태)를 만들다, 형성하다

We **formed** a new debate club / at school.
우리는 새로운 토론 클럽을 만들었다 / 학교에서

## love
**9** ~을 사랑하다, 정말 좋아하다

Even adults **love** ice cream.
어른들도 아이스크림을 정말 좋아한다.

## love (to / -ing)
**10** ~하는 것을 좋아하다, 즐기다

I **love** to play soccer / after school.
나는 축구하기를 정말 좋아한다 / 방과 후에

## pronounce
**11** ~을 발음하다

I want to **pronounce** the words / clearly.
나는 단어를 발음하고 싶다 / 명료하게

## publish
**12** ~을 출판하다, 발표하다

The company has **published** many fine books.
그 회사는 많은 좋은 책을 출판했다.

## purchase
**13** ~을 사다, 구입하다, 얻다

We can **purchase** things / from all over the world.
우리는 물건들을 구입할 수 있다 / 세계 각지로부터

## record
**14** ~을 녹음하다, 적어 두다

I **recorded** my song / directly with my cell phone.
나는 내 노래를 녹음했다 / 바로 내 휴대전화기에

## strike
**15** ~을 치다, 때리다

strikes    struck    struck

He **struck** the wall / with his fist.
그는 벽을 쳤다 / 그의 주먹으로

A 빈칸에 알맞은 단어를 〈보기〉에서 찾아 쓰세요.

**1** They _____ first prize to Laura.

그들은 로라에게 일등상을 수여했다.

**2** The fisherman _____ the fish back into the river.

어부는 그 물고기를 다시 강에 던졌다.

**3** Robots can _____ illness in its early stage.

로봇은 병의 초기 단계에서 그것을 발견할 수 있다.

**4** Alexander Fleming _____ penicillin.

알렉산더 플레밍은 페니실린을 발견했다.

**5** The smell _____ me.

그 냄새가 나를 역겹게 한다.

**6** The company will _____ five percent of its employees.

그 회사는 5 퍼센트의 직원을 해고할 것이다.

**7** He _____ his kite in the park.

그는 공원에서 연을 날렸다.

**8** We _____ a new debate club at school.

우리는 학교에서 새로운 토론 클럽을 만들었다.

> **보기**
> cast
> awarded
> disgusts
> dismiss
> flew
> detect
> discovered
> formed

B 단어를 알맞게 배열하여 문장을 완성하세요.

**1**　　love　　　　　　Even adults　　　　　　ice cream.

_____

**2**　　soccer　　　after school.　　　　I　　　　love to play

_____

**3**　　want to pronounce　　　clearly.　　　I　　　the words

_____

**4**　　has published　　　The company　　　many fine books.

_____

**5**　　We　　　things　　　can purchase　　from all over the world.

_____

**6**　　my song　　directly with my cell phone.　　　I　　　recorded

_____

**7**　　the wall　　　He　　　with his fist.　　　struck

_____

C 다음 문장에서 동사를 찾아 동그라미하고, 해석을 써 보세요.

**1** Alexander Fleming discovered penicillin.

_____

**2** Even adults love ice cream.

_____

**3** We can purchase things from all over the world.

_____

**4** He struck the wall with his fist.

_____

**5** The company has published many fine books.

_____

**6** I want to pronounce the words clearly.

_____

**7** He flew his kite in the park.

_____

**8** I recorded my song directly with my cell phone.

_____

**9** The fisherman cast the fish into the river.

_____

**10** I love to play soccer after school.

_____

**11** We formed a new debate club at school.

_____

**12** The smell disgusts me.

_____

**13** Robots can detect illness in its early stage.

_____

**14** The company will dismiss five percent of its employees.

_____

**15** They awarded first prize to Laura.

_____

| | 3인칭/현재 | 과거 | 과거분사 |
|---|---|---|---|

☐ **await**

1    ~을 기다리다

I **awaited** your call / last night.
나는 너의 전화를 기다렸다 / 어젯밤

☐ **carry**

2    ~을 운반하다, 나르다

Janet **carried** her wooden logs / on her back.
자넷은 나무 목재들을 날랐다 / 자신의 등에 싣고

☐ **desire**

3    ~을 바라다, ~하기를 요구하다

Don **desired** nothing / but fame.
돈은 아무것도 바라지 않았다 / 명성 외에는

☐ **destroy**

4    ~을 무너뜨리다, 파괴하다

The earthquake **destroyed** all of the houses / on our street.
지진은 모든 집들을 무너뜨렸다 / 우리 길에 있는

☐ **disclose**

5    ~을 밝히다, 폭로하다

Teachers have **disclosed** their criminal records.
선생님들은 그들의 범죄 기록을 밝혀 왔다.

☐ **discount**

6    ~을 할인하다

The shop **discounts** ten percent / on all items.
그 가게는 10 퍼센트 할인한다 / 모든 품목을

☐ **fill**

7    ~을 가득 채우다, 가득하게 하다

You can **fill** the jar / with anything you want.
너는 항아리를 채울 수 있다 / 네가 원하는 것 무엇으로든

## get

**8** ~을 받다, 얻다, 벌다, 타다

gets — got — gotten

She **got** a text message / from an unknown number.
그녀는 문자를 받았다 / 알 수 없는 번호로부터

## look

**9** ~으로 보이다, ~인 것 같다

She **looks** like a smart girl.
그녀는 똑똑한 소녀처럼 보인다.

## pray

**10** ~을 기도하다

I'll **pray** Lisa grows up wise and healthy.
나는 리사가 지혜롭고 건강하게 자라길 기도할 것이다.

## prescribe

**11** ~을 처방하다, 지시하다

The doctor **prescribed** a long rest / for me.
의사는 긴 휴식을 처방했다 / 나에게

## push

**12** ~을 밀다, 누르다, 재촉하다

Moana **pushed** her boat / into the sea.
모아나는 그녀의 보트를 밀었다 / 바다로

## recommend

**13** ~을 권하다, 추천하다

I **recommend** this book / for holidays.
나는 이 책을 추천한다 / 휴일을 위해

## sit

**14** ~을 앉히다, (말, 보트 등을) 타다

sits — sat — sat

Grandpa **sat** me / in his favorite chair.
할아버지는 나를 앉혔다 / 그가 가장 좋아하는 의자에

## stretch

**15** ~을 당기다, 뻗치다

I **stretched** myself out / on the ground.
나는 몸을 뻗고 누웠다 / 바닥에

# Mini Test

A 빈칸에 알맞은 단어를 〈보기〉에서 찾아 쓰세요.

**1** I _____ your call last night.

나는 어젯밤 너의 전화를 기다렸다.

**2** Janet _____ her wooden logs on her back.

나무 목재들을 자신의 등에 싣고 날랐다.

**3** Don _____ nothing but fame.

돈은 명성 외에는 아무것도 바라지 않았다.

**4** The earthquake _____ all of the houses on our street.

지진은 우리 길에 있는 모든 집들을 무너뜨렸다.

**5** Teachers have _____ their criminal records.

선생님들은 그들의 범죄 기록을 밝혀야 한다.

**6** The shop _____ ten percent on all items.

그 가게는 모든 품목을 10 퍼센트 할인한다.

**7** You can _____ the jar with anything you want.

너는 내가 원하는 무엇으로든 항아리를 채울 수 있다.

**8** She _____ a text message from an unknown number.

그녀는 알 수 없는 번호로부터 문자를 받았다.

| 보기 |
| --- |
| fill |
| carried |
| awaited |
| destroyed |
| disclosed |
| got |
| discounts |
| desired |

B 단어를 알맞게 배열하여 문장을 완성하세요.

**1** looks like       She       a smart girl.

_____

**2** I'll       Lisa grows up       pray       wise and healthy.

_____

**3** prescribed       The doctor       a long rest       for me.

_____

**4** pushed       into the sea.       Moana       her boat

_____

**5** I       this book       recommend       for holidays.

_____

**6** sat       Grandpa       in his favorite chair.       me

_____

**7** myself       stretched       I       out on the ground.

_____

C 다음 문장에서 동사를 찾아 동그라미하고, 해석을 써 보세요.

**1** I recommend this book for holidays.

_____

**2** I stretched myself out on the ground.

_____

**3** Grandpa sat me in his favorite chair.

_____

**4** Moana pushed her boat into the sea.

_____

**5** The doctor prescribed a long rest for me.

_____

**6** I'll pray Lisa grows up wise and healthy.

_____

**7** You can fill the jar with anything you want.

_____

**8** She looks like a smart girl.

_____

**9** She got a text message from an unknown number.

_____

**10** The shop discounts ten percent on all items.

_____

**11** Teachers have disclosed their criminal records.

_____

**12** The earthquake destroyed all of the houses on our street.

_____

**13** I awaited your call last night.

_____

**14** Don desired nothing but fame.

_____

**15** Janet carried her wooden logs on her back.

_____

| | 3인칭/현재 | 과거 | 과거분사 |
|---|---|---|---|

☐ **attach**

1 ~을 붙이다

You should **attach** a copy of the document.
너는 그 문서의 사본을 첨부해야 한다.

☐ **confront**

2 ~에 맞서다, ~이 닥치다

They **confronted** a thief / with evidence of his crime.
그들은 도둑에 맞섰다 / 그의 범죄의 증거를 가지고

☐ **consult**

3 ~와 상담하다

I will **consult** my teacher / on this question.
나는 우리 선생님과 상담할 것이다 / 이 문제를

☐ **demonstrate**

4 ~을 증명하다, 설명하다

John Dalton **demonstrated** the existence of the atom.
존 달튼은 원자의 존재를 증명했다.

☐ **deserve**

5 ~을 받을 자격이 있다

You **deserve** all of the praise.
너는 모든 칭찬을 받을 자격이 있다.

■ **dig**

6 (땅)을 파다

| digs | dug | dug |

My dog often **digs** the ground.
우리 개는 종종 땅을 판다.

☐ **extend**

7 ~을 펼치다, 연장하다, 뻗다

Government **extends** help / to older workers.
정부는 도움을 펼쳤다 / 나이든 노동자들에게

■ **have**

8    ~을 가지다, (가지고) 있다      has       had       had

I **have** the newest cell phone / in my class.
나는 가장 최신 휴대전화를 가지고 있다 / 우리 반에서

☐ **like**

9    ~을 좋아하다

Everybody **likes** me!
모두 나를 좋아해!

☐ **like (to / -ing)**

10    ~하고 싶어하다

She **likes** to buy new clothes.
그녀는 새 옷을 사는 것을 좋아한다.

☐ **raise**

11    ~을 들어 올리다, (자식을) 키우다

**Raise** your head.
고개를 들어라.

☐ **rank**

12    (순위를) 매기다

This magazine **ranked** Jules above Sina.
이 잡지는 줄을 시나 위로 순위를 매겼다.

☐ **reach**

13    ~에 이르다, 닿다

Humans can **reach** the Sun / by the 2060s.
인간은 태양에 닿을 수 있다 / 2060년대에는

☐ **solve**

14    ~을 해결하다, 풀다

Can you **solve** this problem?
너는 이 문제를 해결할 수 있니?

☐ **study**

15    ~을 공부하다, 배우다

She has **studied** the universe / all her life.
그녀는 우주를 공부했다 / 평생 동안

# Mini Test

A 빈칸에 알맞은 단어를 〈보기〉에서 찾아 쓰세요.

**1** You should _____ a copy of the document.
너는 그 문서의 사본을 첨부해야 한다.

**2** They _____ a thief with evidence of his crime.
그들은 도둑의 범죄의 증거를 가지고 도둑에 맞섰다.

**3** I will _____ my teacher on this question.
나는 우리 선생님과 이 문제를 상담할 것이다.

**4** John Dalton _____ the existence of the atom.
존 달튼은 원자의 존재를 증명했다.

**5** You _____ all of the praise.
너는 모든 칭찬을 받을 자격이 있다.

**6** My dog often _____ the ground.
우리 개는 종종 땅을 판다.

**7** Government _____ help to older workers.
정부는 나이든 노동자들에게 도움을 펼쳤다.

**8** I _____ the newest cell phone in my class.
나는 우리 반에서 가장 최신 휴대전화를 가지고 있다.

보기

attach
consult
confronted
deserve
demonstrated
extends
digs
have

B 단어를 알맞게 배열하여 문장을 완성하세요.

**1** Everybody     me!     likes

_____

**2** likes to     She     buy new clothes.

_____

**3** your     Raise     head.

_____

**4** ranked     This magazine     Jules above Sina.

_____

**5** Humans     the Sun     by the 2060s.     can reach

_____

**6** Can you     this problem?     solve

_____

**7** the universe     all her life.     She     has studied

_____

C 다음 문장에서 동사를 찾아 동그라미하고, 해석을 써 보세요.

**1** Everybody likes me!

_____

**2** Raise your head.

_____

**3** She likes to buy new clothes.

_____

**4** She has studied the universe all her life.

_____

**5** Can you solve this problem?

_____

**6** Humans can reach the Sun by the 2060s.

_____

**7** Government extends help to older workers.

_____

**8** They confronted a thief with evidence of his crime.

_____

**9** You should attach a copy of the document.

_____

**10** I will consult my teacher on this question.

_____

**11** I have the newest cell phone in my class.

_____

**12** This magazine ranked Jules above Sina.

_____

**13** My dog often digs the ground.

_____

**14** You deserve all of the praise.

_____

**15** John Dalton demonstrated the existence of the atom.

_____

MP3

| | 3인칭/현재 | 과거 | 과거분사 |
|---|---|---|---|

☐ **assure**
1 ~을 보장하다

They **assured** that idol group's success.
그들은 저 아이돌 그룹의 성공을 보장했다.

☐ **confine**
2 ~을 한정하다, 가두다

Police **confine** thieves / in prison.
경찰은 도둑들을 가둔다 / 감옥에

☐ **consume**
3 ~을 소비하다, 마구 쓰다, 먹다

We **consume** lots of time / on mobile devices.
우리는 많은 시간을 소비한다 / 모바일 기기에

☐ **decorate**
4 ~을 장식하다, 꾸미다

We **decorate** our Christmas tree / in November every year.
우리는 크리스마스 트리를 장식한다 / 매년 11월에

☐ **delete**
5 ~을 삭제하다

I've **deleted** all the photos / from my cell phone.
나는 모든 사진을 지웠다 / 내 휴대전화기에 있는

☐ **deliver**
6 ~을 배달하다, 전하다

The postman **delivers** the mail / early in the morning.
그 우편배달부는 편지를 배달한다 / 아침 일찍

☐ **express**
7 ~을 나타내다

People **express** their emotions / using languages.
사람들은 그들의 감정을 표현한다 / 언어를 사용하여

194

**help**

8 ~을 돕다, 거들다

He always **helps** his mom / with the housework.
그는 항상 자신의 엄마를 돕는다 / 집안일로

**leave**  leaves  left  left

9 ~을 떠나다

The train **leaves** Busan / at 3.
그 기차는 부산을 떠난다 / 3시에

**live**

10 ~한 생활을 하다

Tom **lived** a life of ease.
톰은 편한 생활을 했다.

**realize**

11 ~을 깨닫다

She didn't **realize** how much she missed him.
그녀는 그녀가 그를 얼마나 그리워하는지 깨닫지 못했다.

**sign**

12 ~을 서명하다, 승인하다

Please **sign** your name / here.
당신의 이름을 서명해 주세요 / 여기에

**supply**

13 ~을 공급하다, 제공하다

Schools should **supply** textbooks / for all students.
학교는 교과서를 공급해야 한다 / 모든 학생에게

**take**  takes  took  taken

14 ~을 가지고 가다, 가져다 주다, 데리고 가다

He **took** his pet dog / to school.
그는 자신의 반려견을 데리고 갔다 / 학교에

**think**  thinks  thought  thought

15 ~라고 생각하다

He **thought** that it was true.
그는 그것이 사실이라고 생각했다.

**A** 빈칸에 알맞은 단어를 〈보기〉에서 찾아 쓰세요.

**1** They _____ that idol group's success.
그들은 저 아이돌 그룹의 성공을 보장했다.

**2** Police _____ thieves in prison.
경찰은 도둑들을 감옥에 가둔다.

**3** We _____ lots of time on mobile devices.
우리는 모바일 기기에 많은 시간을 소비한다.

**4** We _____ our Christmas tree in November every year.
우리는 매년 11월에 크리스마스 트리를 장식한다.

**5** I've _____ all the photos from my cell phone.
나는 내 휴대전화기에 있는 모든 사진을 지웠다.

**6** The postman _____ the mail early in the morning.
그 우편배달부는 아침 일찍 편지를 배달한다.

**7** People _____ their emotions using languages.
사람들은 감정을 언어를 사용하여 표현한다.

**8** He always _____ his mom with the housework.
그는 항상 집안일로 자신의 엄마를 돕는다.

보기
assured
decorate
consume
confine
deleted
express
delivers
helps

**B** 단어를 알맞게 배열하여 문장을 완성하세요.

**1** Busan / The train / leaves / at 3.

**2** lived / Tom / a life of ease.

**3** didn't realize / she missed him. / She / how much

**4** Please / your name here. / sign

**5** Schools / textbooks / for all students. / should supply

**6** took / his pet dog / He / to school.

**7** He / that it was true. / thought

C 다음 문장에서 동사를 찾아 동그라미하고, 해석을 써 보세요.

1 Please sign your name here.
_____

2 The train leaves Busan at 3.
_____

3 Tom lived a life of ease.
_____

4 He thought that it was true.
_____

5 Schools should supply textbooks for all students.
_____

6 He took his pet dog to school.
_____

7 People don't know how to express their emotions.
_____

8 She didn't realize how much she missed him.
_____

9 They assured that idol group's success.
_____

10 We consume lots of time on mobile devices.
_____

11 The postman delivers the mail early in the morning.
_____

12 Police confine thieves in prison.
_____

13 I've deleted all the photos from my cell phone.
_____

14 He always helps his mom with the housework.
_____

15 We decorate our Christmas tree in November every year.
_____

| | 3인칭/현재 | 과거 | 과거분사 |
|---|---|---|---|

**attain**

1  ~을 이루다, 달성하다

Mirea School **attained** the highest score / in 2017.
미래 학교는 가장 높은 점수를 기록했다 / 2017년에

**connect**

2  ~을 연결하다, 접속시키다

We **connected** the two towns / with a bridge.
우리는 두 마을을 연결했다 / 다리로

**deny**

3  ~을 사실이 아니라고 말하다, 부인하다

Ron **denied** eating my cookies.
론은 내 쿠키를 먹은 것을 부인했다.

**describe**

4  ~을 묘사하다

Can you **describe** your pain / to the doctor?
네 통증을 묘사할 수 있니 / 의사에게?

**diminish**

5  ~을 줄이다, 약화시키다

This law would **diminish** social diversity.
이 법은 사회적 다양성을 약화시킬 것이다

**dip**

6  ~을 살짝 담그다

**Dip** your fingers / into a bowl of water.
네 손가락을 담구어라 / 물 그릇에

**feed**　　　　　　feeds　　　fed　　　fed

7  ~에 밥을 주다, 먹이를 주다

Please do not **feed** wild animals.
야생 동물에게 먹이를 주지 마세요.

### give
**8** ~을 주다

gives     gave     given

Grandma **gave** a watch / to me.
할머니는 시계를 주셨다 / 나에게

### lead
**9** ~을 안내하다, 이끌다

leads     led     led

Guide dogs **lead** blind people.
안내견들은 시각장애인을 안내한다.

### pile
**10** ~을 쌓다, 포개다

We had to **pile** the leaves / next to a tree.
우리는 잎을 쌓아야 했다 / 나무 옆에

### pour
**11** (액체)를 붓다, 따르다

She **poured** tea / for me.
그녀는 차를 따랐다 / 나에게

### race
**12** ~과 경주하다, ~을 앞지르려고 달리다

I'll **race** you / for the bathroom.
나는 너와 경주할 것이다 / 화장실까지

### scold
**13** ~를 꾸짖다

My parents **scolded** me / for lying.
우리 부모님은 나를 꾸짖었다 / 거짓말한 것에 대해

### stop
**14** ~을 멈추게 하다, 그만두다

A girl **stopped** the thief.
소녀는 그 도둑을 멈추게 했다.

# Mini Test

A 빈칸에 알맞은 단어를 〈보기〉에서 찾아 쓰세요.

**1** Mirea School _____ the highest score in 2017.

미래 학교는 2017년에 가장 높은 점수를 기록했다.

**2** We _____ the two towns with a bridge.

우리는 두 마을을 다리로 연결했다.

**3** Ron _____ eating my cookies.

론은 내 쿠키를 먹은 것을 부인했다.

**4** Can you _____ your pain to the doctor?

네 통증을 의사에게 묘사할 수 있니?

**5** This law would _____ social diversity.

이 법은 사회적 다양성을 약화시킬 것이다.

**6** _____ your fingers into a bowl of water.

물 그릇에 네 손가락을 담구어라.

**7** Please do not _____ wild animals.

야생 동물에게 먹이를 주지 마세요.

보기
attained
denied
describe
connected
diminish
feed
Dip

B 단어를 알맞게 배열하여 문장을 완성하세요.

**1**  Grandma       to me.       gave       a watch

_____

**2**  Guide dogs       blind people.       lead

_____

**3**  We       had to pile       next to a tree.       the leaves

_____

**4**  She       poured       for me.       tea

_____

**5**  you       I'll       race       for the bathroom.

_____

**6**  for lying.       scolded       me       My parents

_____

**7**  stopped       A girl       the thief.

_____

C 다음 문장에서 동사를 찾아 동그라미하고, 해석을 써 보세요.

**1** She poured tea for me.

_____

**2** Guide dogs lead blind people.

_____

**3** A girl stopped the thief.

_____

**4** Can you describe your pain to the doctor?

_____

**5** This law would diminish social diversity.

_____

**6** Dip your fingers into a bowl of water.

_____

**7** Please do not feed wild animals.

_____

**8** Grandma gave a watch to me.

_____

**9** We connected the two towns with a bridge.

_____

**10** We had to pile the leaves next to a tree.

_____

**11** Mirea School attained the highest score in 2017.

_____

**12** I'll race you for the bathroom.

_____

**13** My parents scolded me for lying.

_____

**14** Ron denied eating my cookies.

_____

MP3

| | 3인칭/현재 | 과거 | 과거분사 |
|---|---|---|---|

☐ **assert**

1  ~을 강력히 주장하다

The lawyer will **assert** his client's innocence.
변호사는 그의 의뢰인의 무죄를 강력히 주장할 것이다.

☐ **contradict**

2  ~을 반박하다, 부정하다

Nobody can **contradict** this statement.
아무도 이 진술을 부정할 수 없다.

☐ **convince**

3  ~에게 납득시키다, ~라고 믿게 하다

The prosecutor **convinced** a jury / of the thief's guilt.
검사는 배심원들에게 납득시켰다 / 도둑의 죄에 대해

☐ **cultivate**

4  ~을 경작하다, 일구다

The farmer has **cultivated** the field / all of his life.
그 농부는 땅을 일궜다 / 그의 평생

☐ **declare**

5  ~을 선언하다, 공표하다

The mayor **declared** a state of emergency / in the city.
그 시장은 비상사태를 선언했다 / 도시의

☐ **delay**

6  ~을 늦어지게 하다, 지연시키다

Heavy rains **delayed** all flights / at Incheon airport.
폭우가 모든 항공편을 지연시켰다 / 인천 공항에 있는

☐ **export**

7  ~을 수출하다

Canada **exports** grains.
캐나다는 곡식을 수출한다.

## hold
**8** ~을 잡다, 쥐다, (팔에) 안다

holds    held    held

She **held** a one-year-old baby's hand.
그녀는 한 살짜리 아기의 손을 잡았다.

## influence
**9** ~에 영향을 주다

Media **influences** children's behavior.
미디어는 아이들의 행동에 영향을 준다.

## know
**10** ~을 알다

knows    knew    known

Jamie didn't **know** the car was coming.
제이미는 그 차가 오고 있는지 몰랐다.

## recall
**11** ~을 기억해 내다, 상기시키다

He couldn't **recall** the name of his co-worker.
그는 자신의 동료의 이름을 기억해 낼 수 없었다.

## shut
**12** ~을 닫다, 감다, 덮다

shuts    shut    shut

**Shut** your book and notes.
네 책과 공책을 덮어라.

## support
**13** ~을 지지하다, 후원하다

Please **support** our campaign / to help the elderly.
우리 캠페인을 지지해 주세요 / 노인을 돕기 위한

## tell
**14** ~을 말하다

tells    told    told

I **told** the story / to my friend yesterday.
나는 그 이야기를 말했다 / 내 친구에게 어제

# Mini Test

A 빈칸에 알맞은 단어를 〈보기〉에서 찾아 쓰세요.

**1** The lawyer will _____ his client's innocence.

변호사는 그의 의뢰인의 무죄를 강력히 주장할 것이다.

**2** Nobody can _____ this statement.

아무도 이 진술을 부정할 수 없다.

**3** The prosecutor _____ a jury of the thief's guilt.

검사는 도둑의 죄에 대해 배심원들에게 납득시켰다.

**4** The farmer has _____ the field all of his life.

그 농부는 그의 평생 땅을 일궜다.

**5** The mayor _____ a state of emergency in the city.

그 시장은 도시의 비상사태를 선언했다.

**6** Heavy rains _____ all flights at Incheon airport.

폭우가 인천 공항에 모든 항공편을 지연시켰다.

**7** Canada _____ grains.

캐나다는 곡식을 수출한다.

| 보기 |
| --- |
| contradict |
| cultivated |
| assert |
| delayed |
| exports |
| declared |
| convinced |

B 단어를 알맞게 배열하여 문장을 완성하세요.

**1**  held          She          a one-year-old baby's hand.

_____

**2**  Media          children's behavior.          influences

_____

**3**  didn't know          the car was coming.          Jamie

_____

**4**  couldn't recall          He          the name of his co-worker.

_____

**5**  your book          and notes.          Shut

_____

**6**  our campaign          Please support          to help the elderly.

_____

**7**  I          to my friend yesterday.          the story          told

_____

C 다음 문장에서 동사를 찾아 동그라미하고, 해석을 써 보세요.

1 Please support our campaign to help the elderly.
_____

2 Shut your book and notes.
_____

3 Media influences children's behavior.
_____

4 She held a one-year-old baby's hand.
_____

5 The mayor declared a state of emergency in the city.
_____

6 Heavy rains delayed all flights at Incheon airport.
_____

7 He couldn't recall the name of his co-worker.
_____

8 The farmer has cultivated the field all of his life.
_____

9 The prosecutor convinced a jury of the thief's guilt.
_____

10 Jamie didn't know the car was coming.
_____

11 Canada exports grains.
_____

12 Nobody can contradict this statement.
_____

13 The lawyer will assert his client's innocence.
_____

14 I told the story to my friend yesterday.
_____

Pattern 04

## 주어 + 동사 + 간접목적어 + 직접목적어

| 주어 | 동사 | 간접목적어 (~에게) | 직접목적어 (~을) |
|------|------|------------------|------------------|
| I<br>나는 | gave<br>주었다 | him<br>그에게 | the book.<br>그 책을 |
| He<br>그는 | taught<br>가르쳤다 | me<br>나에게 | English.<br>영어를 |

타동사 give는 '~을 주다'라는 뜻이라고 앞에서 배웠어요. 이번에는 '~에게 ~을 주다'라는 뜻의 give 동사를 배워 봐요. 이때는 「~에게」와 「~을」에 해당하는 '목적어'가 두 개 있어야 완전한 의미의 문장을 만들 수 있어요.

Tip. 동사 하나로 같은 의미의 문장 2개 만들기

\* 동사에 따라 바뀌는 전치사를 눈여겨 보세요!

I **handed** my mom the bag.
= I **handed** the bag **to** my mom.
나는 엄마에게 가방을 건넸다.

She **asked** me a question.
= She **asked** a question **of** me.
그녀는 나에게 질문을 했다.

We'll **make** you a house.
= We'll **make** a house **for** you.
우리는 너에게 집을 만들어 줄 것이다.

## Day 49

MP3

| | 3인칭/현재 | 과거 | 과거분사 |
|---|---|---|---|

**☐ 1 award**
~에게 ~을 주다, 수여하다

The judge **awarded** me first prize.
심사 위원은 나에게 일등상을 주었다.

= The judge **awarded** first prize **to** me.

**■ 2 give**   gives   gave   given
~에게 ~을 주다

I **gave** you my notebook.
나는 너에게 내 공책을 주었다.

= I **gave** my notebook **to** you.

**☐ 3 guarantee**
~에게 ~을 보장하다

Does a degree **guarantee** you a good job?
학위가 너에게 좋은 직업을 보장하니?

= Does a degree **guarantee** a good job **for** you?

**■ 4 lend**   lends   lent   lent
~에게 ~을 빌려주다

Would you **lend** me your books, please?
나에게 네 책들을 빌려줄래?

= Would you **lend** your books **to** me, please?

**☐ 5 mail**
~에게 ~을 우편으로 부치다

Ken **mailed** his brother a parcel.
켄은 그의 형에게 소포를 우편으로 부쳤다.

= Ken **mailed** a parcel **to** his brother.

208

☐ **offer**
6  ~에게 ~을 제공하다

They **offered** their customers the best product.
그들은 고객에게 최고의 상품을 제공했다.

= They **offered** the best product **to** their customers.


☐ **order**
7  ~에게 ~을 주문하다, 지시하다

My doctor **ordered** me some pills.
의사선생님이 나에게 약간의 약을 처방했다.

= My doctor **ordered** some pills **for** me.


☐ **owe**
8  ~에게 ~을 빚지다

I **owed** him my life.
나는 그에게 내 목숨을 빚졌다.

= I **owed** my life **to** him.


☐ **pour**
9  ~에게 (액체를) 따라주다

She **poured** me a cup of tea.
그녀는 나에게 차 한 잔을 따라주었다.

= She **poured** a cup of tea **for** me.


☐ **promise**
10  ~에게 ~을 약속하다, 계약하다

I **promise** you I won't lie anymore.
나는 너에게 더 이상 거짓말하지 않을 것을 약속한다.

= I **promise** I won't lie anymore **for** you.

A 빈칸에 알맞은 단어를 〈보기〉에서 찾아 쓰세요.

**1** The judge _____ me first prize.

심사 위원은 나에게 일등상을 주었다.

**2** I _____ you my notebook.

나는 너에게 내 공책을 주었다.

**3** Does a degree _____ you a good job?

학위가 너에게 좋은 직업을 보장하니?

**4** Would you _____ me your books, please?

나에게 네 책들을 빌려줄래?

**5** Ken _____ his brother a parcel.

켄은 그의 형에게 소포를 우편으로 부쳤다.

보기
awarded
mailed
gave
lend
guarantee

B 단어를 알맞게 배열하여 문장을 완성하세요.

**1** They     their customers     offered     the best product.

_____

**2** ordered     My doctor     me     some pills.

_____

**3** I     him     owed     my life.

_____

**4** me     She     poured     a cup of tea.

_____

**5** you     I     promise     I won't like anymore.

_____

C 두 문장의 뜻이 같도록 빈칸을 채우고, 해석을 써 보세요.

1 The judge awarded me first prize.

= The judge _____.

_____

2 I gave you my notebook.

= I gave _____.

_____

3 Does a degree guarantee you a good job?

= Does a degree _____?

_____

4 Would you lend me your books, please?

= Would you lend _____?

_____

5 Ken mailed his brother a parcel.

= Ken _____.

_____

6 They offered their customers the best product.

= They offered _____.

_____

7 My doctor ordered me some pills.

= My doctor _____.

_____

8 I owed him my life.

= I owed _____.

_____

9 She poured me a cup of tea.

= She poured _____.

_____

10 I promise you I won't lie anymore.

= I promise I _____.

_____

---

Day **50**

MP3

| | 3인칭/현재 | 과거 | 과거분사 |
|---|---|---|---|

**1. bring**
~에게 (물건을) 가져오다, (사람을) 데려오다

brings   brought   brought

I'll **bring** you the magazine.
내가 너에게 그 잡지를 가져다줄게.
= I'll **bring** the magazine **to** you.

**2. cook**
~에게 ~을 요리해 주다

He **cooked** his wife dinner.
그는 자신의 아내에게 저녁을 요리해 주었다.
= He **cooked** dinner **for** his wife.

**3. charge**
~에게 ~을 청구하다

The library will **charge** me a 5-dollar late fee.
도서관은 나에게 5달러 연체료를 청구할 것이다.
• 문장 변형 없음

**4. do**
~에게 ~을 해주다, 베풀다

does   did   done

Would you **do** me a favor?
내 부탁을 들어주겠니?
= Would you **do** a favor **for** me?

**5. get**
~에게 ~을 가져다주다, 사 주다, 구해 주다

gets   got   gotten

Why don't you **get** her a coat?
그녀에게 코트를 가져다주는 게 어때?
= Why don't you **get** a coat **for** her?

212

### refuse
**6** ~에게 ~을 거절하다, 거부하다

The embassy **refused** him a visa.
대사관은 그에게 비자발급을 거절했다.

= The embassy **refused** a visa **for** him.

### sell
**7** ~에게 ~을 팔다

sells     sold     sold

They **sold** me this carpet.
그들은 나에게 카펫을 팔았다.

=They **sold** this carpet **to** me.

### take
**8** ~에게 ~을 가져다주다

takes     took     taken

They **took** Mia some food.
그들은 미아에게 음식을 가져다주었다.

=They **took** some food **for** Mia.

### tell
**9** ~에게 ~을 알리다, 말하다

tells     told     told

I **told** him my secret.
나는 그에게 나의 비밀을 말했다.

= I **told** my secret **to** him.

### throw
**10** ~에게 ~을 던지다

throws     threw     thrown

I **threw** him a curve ball.
나는 그에게 변화구를 던졌다.

= I **threw** a curve ball **to** him.

A 빈칸에 알맞은 단어를 〈보기〉에서 찾아 쓰세요.

**1** I'll _____ you the magazine.

내가 너에게 그 잡지를 가져다줄게.

**2** He _____ his wife dinner.

그는 자신의 아내에게 저녁을 요리해 주었다.

**3** The library will _____ me a 5-dollar late fee.

도서관은 나에게 5달러 연체료를 청구할 것이다.

**4** Would you _____ me a favor?

내 부탁을 들어주겠니?

**5** Why don't you _____ her a coat?

그녀에게 코트를 가져다주는 게 어때?

| 보기 |
| :---: |
| bring |
| get |
| charge |
| cooked |
| do |

B 단어를 알맞게 배열하여 문장을 완성하세요.

**1** refused       The embassy       him       a visa.

_____

**2** They       me       sold       this carpet.

_____

**3** They       took       some food.       Mia

_____

**4** him       told       I       my secret.

_____

**5** threw       I       him       a curve ball.

_____

C 두 문장의 뜻이 같도록 빈칸을 채우고, 해석을 써 보세요. (문장 변형 없는 것은 해석만)

**1** I'll bring you the magazine.

= I'll bring _____ .

_____

**2** He cooked his wife dinner.

= He cooked _____ .

_____

**3** The library will charge me a 5-dollar late fee.

_____

**4** Would you do me a favor?

= Would you do _____ ?

_____

**5** Why don't you get her a coat?

= Why don't you get _____ ?

_____

**6** The embassy refused him a visa.

= The embassy refused _____ .

_____

**7** They sold me this carpet.

= They sold _____ .

_____

**8** I threw him a curve ball.

= I threw _____ .

_____

**9** I told him my secret.

= I told _____ .

_____

**10** They took Mia some food.

= They took _____ .

_____

**Day 51**

MP3

| | 3인칭/현재 | 과거 | 과거분사 |
|---|---|---|---|

☐ **hand**

1 ~에게 ~을 건네주다, 돌리다

Please **hand** me the cup.
나에게 그 컵을 건네주세요.

= Please **hand** the cup **to** me.


☐ **loan**

2 ~에게 ~을 빌려주다, 대출해 주다

I **loaned** her my dress.
나는 그녀에게 드레스를 빌려줬다.

= I **loaned** my dress **to** her.


☐ **pass**

3 ~에게 ~을 전달하다

**Pass** me the salt, please.
나에게 그 소금을 전달해주세요.

= **Pass** the salt **to** me, please.


■ **pay**           pays           paid           paid

4 ~에게 (얼마를) 지불하다

We will **pay** you 6,000 won an hour.
우리는 너에게 시간당 육천 원을 지불할 것이다.

= We will **pay** 6,000 won an hour **to** you.


☐ **play**

5 ~에게 (음악을) 틀다, 들려주다

Could I **play** you some music?
음악을 들려줄까?

= Could I **play** some music **for** you?

216

### ■ read
6 ~에게 ~을 읽어 주다

reads    read[red]    read[red]

I've **read** my kids interesting stories.
나는 우리 아이들에게 재미있는 이야기를 읽어 줬다.

= I've **read** interesting stories **to** my kids.

### ■ send
7 ~에게 ~을 보내다

sends    sent    sent

I've **sent** my friends postcards / from all my trips.
나는 친구들에게 우편엽서를 보냈다 / 모든 여행에서

= I've **sent** postcards **to** my friends / from all my trips.

### ■ show
8 ~에게 ~을 보여주다

shows    showed    showed/ shown

**Show** me your ticket, please.
저에게 표를 보여주세요.

= **Show** your ticket **to** me, please.

### ■ teach
9 ~에게 ~을 가르치다

teaches    taught    taught

She **taught** us English.
그녀는 우리에게 영어를 가르쳤다.

= She **taught** English **to** us.

### ■ write
10 ~에게 ~을 써 주다

writes    wrote    written

I **wrote** him a song.
나는 그에게 노래를 써 줬다.

= I **wrote** a song **for** him.

A 빈칸에 알맞은 단어를 〈보기〉에서 찾아 쓰세요.

1 Please _____ me the cup.

   나에게 그 컵을 건네주세요.

2 I _____ her my dress.

   나는 그녀에게 드레스를 빌려줬다.

3 _____ me the salt, please.

   나에게 그 소금을 전달해주세요.

4 We will _____ you 6,000 won an hour.

   우리는 너에게 시간당 육천 원을 지불할 것이다.

5 Could I _____ you some music?

   음악을 들려줄까?

> 보기
>
> hand
> pay
> play
> loaned
> Pass

B 단어를 알맞게 배열하여 문장을 완성하세요.

1   read        my kids        I        interesting stories        every night.

   _____

2   I've        postcards from all my trips.        my friends        sent

   _____

3        Show                your ticket, please.                me

   _____

4        us                She                taught                English.

   _____

5        I                wrote                a song.                him

   _____

**C** 두 문장의 뜻이 같도록 빈칸을 채우고, 해석을 써 보세요.

**1** Please hand me the cup.

= Please hand _____.

_____

**2** Pass me the salt, please.

= Pass _____.

_____

**3** We will pay you 6,000 won an hour.

= We will pay _____.

_____

**4** Could I play you some music?

= Could I play _____?

_____

**5** I've read my kids interesting stories.

= I've read _____.

_____

**6** I've sent my friends postcards from all my trips.

= I've sent _____.

_____

**7** Show me your ticket, please.

= Show _____.

_____

**8** She taught us English.

= She taught _____.

_____

**9** I loaned her my dress.

= I loaned _____.

_____

**10** I wrote him a song.

= I wrote _____.

_____

MP3

|  | 3인칭/현재 | 과거 | 과거분사 |
|---|---|---|---|

☐ **ask**
1 ~에게 ~을 물어보다, 부탁하다

He **asked** Lisa where she shops.
그는 리사에게 그녀가 쇼핑하는 곳을 물어봤다.

= He **asked** where she shops **to** Lisa.

■ **buy** — buys — bought — bought
2 ~에게 ~을 사다 주다

Dylan **bought** his brother a CD.
딜런은 그의 동생에게 음반을 사다 줬다.

= Dylan **bought** a CD **for** his brother.

■ **cost** — costs — cost — cost
3 ~에게 (얼마를) 쓰게 하다

The shoes **cost** me 50,000 won.
그 신발은 나에게 오만 원을 쓰게 했다.
• 문장 변형 없음

☐ **inform**
4 ~에게 ~을 알리다

They **informed** me that I won the first prize.
그들은 내게 일등상을 받았다고 알려주었다.
• 문장 변형 없음

■ **find** — finds — found — found
5 ~에게 ~을 찾아 주다

She **found** her student a notebook.
그녀는 자신의 학생에게 공책을 찾아 줬다.

= She **found** a notebook **for** her student.

## grant
**6** ~에게 ~을 허가하다, 승인하다

She **granted** me an interview.
그녀는 나에게 인터뷰를 허가했다.

= She **granted** an interview **to** me.

## make
**7** ~에게 ~을 만들어 주다

makes     made     made

My dad **made** me a kite.
우리 아빠는 나에게 연을 만들어 줬다.

= My dad **made** a kite **for** me.

## save
**8** ~을 위해 ~을 남겨 두다, 저축하다

Jake's parents **saved** him a seat.
제이크의 부모님은 제이크를 위해 좌석을 마련했다.

= Jake's parents **saved** a seat **for** him.

## warn
**9** ~에게 ~을 경고하다

She **warned** us that the floor was wet.
그녀는 우리에게 바닥이 미끄럽다고 경고했다.

= She **warned** that the floor was wet **to** us.

## wish
**10** ~에게 ~을 빌다, 빌어 주다

We **wish** her good luck.
우리는 그녀에게 행운을 빈다.

= We **wish** good luck **to** her.

# Mini Test

**A** 빈칸에 알맞은 단어를 〈보기〉에서 찾아 쓰세요.

**1** He _____ Lisa where she shops.

그는 리사에게 그녀가 쇼핑하는 곳을 물어봤다.

**2** Dylan _____ his brother a CD.

딜란은 그의 동생에게 음반을 사다 줬다.

**3** The shoes _____ me 50,000 won.

그 신발은 나에게 오만 원을 쓰게 했다.

**4** They _____ me that I won the first prize.

그들은 내게 일등상을 받았다고 알려줬다.

보기
asked
cost
bought
informed
found

**5** She _____ her student a notebook.

그녀는 자신의 학생에게 공책을 찾아줬다.

**B** 단어를 알맞게 배열하여 문장을 완성하세요.

**1** me          an interview.          granted          She

_____

**2** made          me          My dad          a kite.

_____

**3** him          Jake's parents          saved          a seat.

_____

**4** warned          She          that the floor was wet.          us

_____

**5** We          good luck.          wish          her

_____

**C** 두 문장의 뜻이 같도록 빈칸을 채우고, 해석을 써 보세요. (문장 변형 없는 것은 해석만)

**1** I'll ask Lisa where she shops.

= I'll ask _____ .

_____

**2** Dylan bought his brother a CD.

= Dylan bought _____ .

_____

**3** The shoes cost me 50,000 won.

_____

**4** They informed me that I won the first prize.

_____

**5** She found her student a notebook.

= She found _____ .

_____

**6** She warned us that the floor was wet.

= She warned _____

**7** She granted me an interview.

= She granted _____ .

_____

**8** My dad made me a kite.

= My dad _____ .

_____

**9** Jake's parents saved him a seat.

= Jake's parents saved _____ .

_____

**10** We wish her good luck.

= We wish _____ .

_____

Pattern 05

# 주어 + 동사 + 목적어 + 목적보어

| 주어 | 동사 | 목적어 | 목적보어 |
|------|------|--------|----------|
| He<br>그는 | found<br>알게 됐다 | the book<br>그 책이 | interesting.<br>재미있다는 것을 |
| We<br>우리는 | call<br>부른다 | New York<br>뉴욕을 | the Big Apple.<br>빅애플이라고 |

find는 '~을 찾다'라는 뜻 말고도 '~이 ~임을 알게 되다'라는 뜻이 있어요. 이때는 뒤에 '~이'에 해당하는 목적어와 이 목적어를 보충 설명해 주는 목적보어가 따라 와요. 위의 문장에서 목적어 the book이 재미있다고 보충해 주는 말 interesting이 바로 목적보어랍니다. 동사에 따라 목적보어 앞에 as, for, of 등의 전치사가 올 수도 있어요.

## Tip. 목적보어로 쓸 수 있는 것들

**1 명사**  My parents made me a pilot. (me = a pilot) 우리 부모님이 나를 비행사로 만들었다.

**2 형용사**  My parents had me happy. (me = happy) 우리 부모님은 나를 행복하게 한다.

**3 to + 동사원형**  My parents wanted me to read books. (me = to read books)
우리 부모님은 내가 책을 읽기를 원했다.

**4 분사**  My parents saw my room cleaned. (my room = cleaned 수동)
우리 부모님은 내 방이 깨끗하게 치워진 것을 보았다.

My parents saw me cleaning my room. (me = cleaning my room 능동)
우리 부모님은 내가 방을 깨끗하게 치운 것을 보았다.

MP3

| | 3인칭/현재 | 과거 | 과거분사 |
|---|---|---|---|

☐ **appoint**

1 ~을 ~으로 지명하다

The students **appointed** Sanho their chairman.
학생들은 산호를 그들의 회장으로 지명했다.

☐ **boil**

2 ~에게 ~을 삶아 주다

My dad **boiled** me an egg / every morning.
우리 아빠는 나에게 계란을 삶아 주었다 / 매일 아침

☐ **call**

3 ~를 ~라고 부르다

We **called** him Uncle Bob.
우리는 그를 밥 삼촌이라고 불렀다.

■ **catch**     catches    caught    caught

4 ~가 ~하는 것을 목격하다

My mom **caught** me playing computer games / again.
우리 엄마는 내가 컴퓨터 게임하는 것을 목격했다 / 또

☐ **consider**

5 ~가 ~라고 생각하다

I **consider** you an expert.
나는 네가 전문가라고 생각한다.

☐ **declare**

6 ~이 ~라고 선언하다

Governors **declared** the drought a disaster.
정부는 가뭄이 재난이라고 선언했다.

■ **find**     finds    found    found

7 ~가 ~임을 알게 되다

She **found** the movie exciting.
그녀는 그 영화가 재미있음을 알게 됐다.

## ■ hear
**8** ~가 ~하는 것이 들리다

hears     heard     heard

I could **hear** a bird singing / in the woods.
나는 새가 노래하는 것을 들을 수 있었다 / 숲에서

## ☐ judge
**9** ~가 ~라고 판단하다, 생각하다

They **judged** Somi arrogant.
그들은 소미가 오만하다고 판단했다.

## ■ keep
**10** ~이 ~하게 유지하다

keeps     kept     kept

We have to **keep** the river clean.
우리는 그 강을 깨끗하게 지켜야만 한다.

## ■ leave
**11** ~가 ~하게 두다

leaves     left     left

He **left** his car unlocked.
그는 그의 차가 열린 채 두었다.

## ■ make
**12** ~를 ~하게 만들다

makes     made     made

The news **made** me happy.
그 뉴스는 나를 행복하게 만들었다.

## ☐ name
**13** ~을 ~라고 이름 짓다

They **named** their daughter Mia.
그들은 그들의 딸을 미아라고 이름 지었다.

## ☐ push
**14** ~이 ~하게 밀다, 누르다

She **pushed** a door open.
그녀는 문이 열리게 밀었다.

## ☐ urge
**15** ~이 ~하도록 충고하다, 촉구하다

Several people **urged** the council members to pass the bills.
많은 사람들은 의원들이 법률을 통과시키도록 촉구했다.

## Mini Test

**A** 빈칸에 알맞은 단어를 〈보기〉에서 찾아 쓰세요.

**1** The students _____ Sanho their chairman.

학생들은 산호를 그들의 회장으로 지명했다.

**2** My dad _____ me an egg every morning.

우리 아빠는 매일 아침 나에게 계란을 삶아 주었다.

**3** We _____ him Uncle Bob.

우리는 그를 밥 삼촌이라고 불렀다.

**4** My mom _____ me playing computer games again.

우리 엄마는 내가 또 컴퓨터 게임하는 것을 목격했다.

**5** I _____ you an expert.

나는 네가 전문가라고 생각한다.

**6** Governors _____ the drought a disaster.

정부는 가뭄이 재난이라고 선언했다.

**7** She _____ the movie exciting.

그녀는 그 영화가 재미있음을 알게 됐다.

**8** I could _____ a bird singing in the woods.

나는 숲에서 새가 노래하는 것을 들을 수 있었다.

> **보기**
>
> called
> boiled
> caught
> appointed
> found
> hear
> consider
> declared

**B** 단어를 알맞게 배열하여 문장을 완성하세요.

**1**  Somi     They     arrogant.     judged

_____

**2**  We     clean.     the river     have to keep

_____

**3**  He     unlocked.     left     his car

_____

**4**  their daughter     They     named     Mia.

_____

**5**  me     made     The news     happy.

_____

**6**  pushed     She     open.     a door

_____

**7**  urged     the council members     Several people     to pass the bills.

_____

C 다음 문장에서 동사를 찾아 동그라미하고, 해석을 써 보세요.

1 He left his car unlocked.
_____

2 We have to keep the river clean.
_____

3 The news made me happy.
_____

4 My mom caught me playing computer games again.
_____

5 They named their daughter Mia.
_____

6 They judged Somi arrogant.
_____

7 She pushed a door open.
_____

8 Governors declared the drought a disaster.
_____

9 I could hear a bird singing in the woods.
_____

10 Several people urged the council members to pass the bills.
_____

11 My dad boiled me an egg every morning.
_____

12 The students appointed Sanho their chairman.
_____

13 I consider you an expert.
_____

14 We called him Uncle Bob.
_____

15 She found the movie exciting.
_____

MP3

| | 3인칭/현재 | 과거 | 과거분사 |
|---|---|---|---|

**☐ advise**
1 ~에게 ~을 충고하다

I have **advised** them not **to** watch TV.
나는 그들에게 텔레비전 보지 않도록 충고했다.

**☐ allow**
2 ~이 ~하는 것을 허락하다

My parents **allowed** me **to** play video games.
우리 부모님은 내가 비디오 게임하는 것을 허락했다.

**☐ desire**
3 ~이 ~하여 주기를 요구하다

I **desire** you **to** leave now.
나는 네가 지금 떠나 주기를 요구한다.

**☐ enable**
4 ~이 ~을 할 수 있게 하다

Smart phones **enable** us **to** know more information.
스마트폰은 우리가 더 많은 정보를 아는 것을 가능하게 한다.

**☐ encourage**
5 ~이 ~을 하게 하다, 장려하다

We **encourage** you **to** take advantage of this.
우리는 네가 이것을 이용하기를 격려한다.

**☐ expect**
6 ~이 ~하기를 기대하다

She **expected** her boyfriend **to** come early.
그녀는 자신의 남자친구가 일찍 올 것을 기대했다.

**■ forbid**                    forbids        forbade        forbid/
7 ~에게 ~을 금하다                                             forbidden

The regulation **forbids** students **to** think differently.
규제는 학생들이 다르게 생각하는 것을 금한다.

## force
8  ~이 ~을 하게 만들다

My teacher **forced** us **to** do homework over our break.
우리 선생님은 우리가 방학 동안 숙제를 하게 만들었다.

## lead
9  ~을 ~로 안내하다

leads     led     led

The secretary **led** the guest **to** the boardroom.
비서가 손님을 회의실로 이끌었다.

## promote
10  ~을 ~로 승진시키다

The firm **promoted** some clerk **to** office manager.
그 회사는 몇몇 점원을 관리인으로 승진시켰다.

## recommend
11  ~에게 ~을 추천하다

Would you **recommend** me **to** read this book?
너는 내가 이 책을 읽는 것을 추천하겠니?

## request
12  ~에게 ~을 요청하다

The school **requested** all students **to** attend classes early.
그 학교는 모든 학생들이 수업에 일찍 참석 하기를 요청했다.

## require
13  ~이 ~할 것을 요구하다

The patients **required** doctors **to** notify them of their situation.
환자들은 의사들이 자신의 상태를 알려줄 것을 요구했다.

## teach
14  ~에게 ~을 가르치다

teaches     taught     taught

I **teach** him **to** study English grammar.
나는 그에게 영어 문법 공부하는 것을 가르친다.

## trade
15  ~을 ~과 교환하다, 거래하다

She **traded** everything **for** the jewelry.
그녀는 모든 것을 보석으로 거래했다.

# Mini Test

**A** 빈칸에 알맞은 단어를 〈보기〉에서 찾아 쓰세요.

**1** I have _____ them not to watch TV.

나는 그들에게 텔레비전 보지 않도록 충고했다.

**2** My parents _____ me to play video games.

우리 부모님은 내가 비디오 게임 하는 것을 허락했다.

**3** I _____ you to leave now.

나는 네가 지금 떠나 주기를 요구한다.

**4** Smart phones _____ us to know more information.

스마트폰은 우리가 더 많은 정보를 아는 것을 가능하게 한다.

**5** We _____ you to take advantage of this.

우리는 네가 이것을 이용하기를 격려한다.

**6** She _____ her boyfriend to come early.

그녀는 자신의 남자친구가 일찍 올 것을 기대했다.

**7** The regulation _____ students to think differently.

규제는 학생들이 다르게 생각하는 것을 금한다.

**8** My teacher _____ us to do homework over our break.

우리 선생님은 우리가 방학 동안 숙제를 하게 만들었다.

> 보기
>
> desire
> advised
> enable
> allowed
> expected
> encourage
> forced
> forbids

**B** 단어를 알맞게 배열하여 문장을 완성하세요.

**1** to the boardroom.　　The secretary　　led　　the guest

_____

**2** The firm　　some clerk　　to office manager.　　promoted

_____

**3** Would you　　me　　recommend　　to read this book?

_____

**4** The school　　to attend classes early.　　requested　　all students

_____

**5** The patients　　doctors　　to notify their situation.　　required

_____

**6** I　　him　　teach　　to study English grammar.

_____

**7** She　　for the jewelry.　　traded　　everything

_____

232

C 다음 문장에서 동사를 찾아 동그라미하고, 해석을 써 보세요.

**1** The regulation forbids students to think differently.

_____

**2** The firm promoted some clerk to office manager.

_____

**3** Would you recommend me to read this book?

_____

**4** The school requested all students to attend classes early.

_____

**5** The patients required doctors to notify their situation.

_____

**6** I teach him to study English grammar.

_____

**7** She traded everything for the jewelry.

_____

**8** The secretary led the guest to the boardroom.

_____

**9** My teacher forced us to do homework over our break.

_____

**10** She expected her boyfriend to come early.

_____

**11** I have advised them not to watch TV.

_____

**12** My parents allowed me to play video games.

_____

**13** I desire you to leave now.

_____

**14** Smart phones enable us to know more information.

_____

**15** We encourage you to take advantage of this.

_____

# Day 55

MP3

| | 3인칭/현재 | 과거 | 과거분사 |
|---|---|---|---|

**1 cause**
~가 ~하게 하다

Heavy rain in Seoul **caused** a river **to** flood.
서울의 폭우가 강을 넘치게 했다.

**2 convince**
~가 ~하게 설득하다

Tina has **convinced** me **to** vote for her.
티나는 내가 그녀 자신을 뽑도록 설득하였다.

**3 elect**
~을 ~으로 뽑다

We **elected** Lisa chairperson.
우리는 리사를 의장으로 뽑았다.

**4 feel**    feels   felt   felt
~이 ~하는 것을 느끼다

We **felt** these donations **to** be helpful.
우리는 이 기증들이 도움이 된다는 것을 느꼈다.

**5 get**    gets   got   gotten
~가 ~하게 하다

I **got** my dog not **to** bark at my neighbors.
나는 우리 개가 이웃들에게 짖지 않게 했다.

**6 instruct**
~에게 ~할 것을 지시하다

The officer **instructed** us not to drop litter.
경찰은 우리에게 쓰레기를 버리지 말 것을 지시했다.

**7 order**
~에게 ~할 것을 명령하다

My mom **ordered** my little brother **to** stop.
엄마는 내 동생에게 멈출 것을 명령했다

234

### persuade
**8** ~에게 ~하도록 설득하다

I tried to **persuade** him **to** see a doctor.
나는 그에게 병원에 가도록 설득하려고 했다.

### remind
**9** ~가 ~하도록 상기시키다

**Remind** me **to** phone Jina at 5.
내가 다섯 시에 지나에게 전화하도록 상기시켜줘.

### ■ tell
**10** ~에게 ~을 시키다, 지시하다

tells     told     told

I **told** you **to** be patient.
나는 네게 참으라고 지시했다.

### ■ think
**11** ~가 ~라고 생각하다

thinks     thought     thought

I **thought** her **to** be attractive.
나는 그녀가 매력적이라고 생각했다.

### trust
**12** ~가 ~할 것을 믿다

I can't **trust** Julie **to** keep my secrets.
나는 줄리가 내 비밀을 지키리라 믿을 수 없다.

### want
**13** ~가 ~하기를 바라다

She **wants** me **to** finish my work on time.
그녀는 내가 일을 제시간에 마치기를 원한다.

### warn
**14** ~에게 ~라고 경고하다

I **warned** you not **to** go there.
나는 너에게 거기 가지 말라고 경고했었다.

### wish
**15** ~가 ~해 주기를 바라다

I **wish** her **to** try her best at school.
나는 그녀가 학교에서 최선을 다하기를 바란다.

A 빈칸에 알맞은 단어를 〈보기〉에서 찾아 쓰세요.

1 Heavy rain in Seoul _____ a river to flood.
서울의 폭우는 강이 넘치게 했다.

2 Tina has _____ me to vote for her.
티나는 내가 그녀를 뽑도록 설득하였다.

3 We _____ Lisa chairperson.
우리는 리사를 의장으로 뽑았다.

4 We _____ these donations to be helpful.
우리는 이 기증들이 도움이 된다는 것을 느꼈다.

5 I _____ my dog not to bark at my neighbors.
나는 우리 개가 이웃들에게 짖지 않게 했다.

6 The officer _____ us not to drop litter.
경찰은 우리가 쓰레기를 버리지 말 것을 지시했다.

7 My mom _____ my little brother to stop.
엄마는 내 동생에게 멈출 것을 명령했다.

8 I tried to _____ him to see a doctor.
나는 그가 병원에 가게 설득하려고 했다.

보기
caused
felt
instructed
got
convinced
persuade
ordered
elected

B 단어를 알맞게 배열하여 문장을 완성하세요.

1 | They | me | to keep silent. | required |

2 | told | you | I | to be patient. |

3 | I | her | thought | to be attractive. |

4 | Julie | to keep my secrets. | I | can't trust |

5 | me | She | wants | my work on time. | to finish |

6 | I | you | not to go there. | warned |

7 | I | to try | wish | her | her best at school. |

C 다음 문장에서 동사를 찾아 동그라미하고, 해석을 써 보세요.

**1** I thought her to be attractive.
_____

**2** She wants me to finish my work on time.
_____

**3** I warned you not to go there.
_____

**4** I can't trust Julie to keep my secrets.
_____

**5** I wish her to try her best at school.
_____

**6** I told you to be patient.
_____

**7** We elected Lisa chairperson.
_____

**8** Remind me to phone Jina at 5.
_____

**9** I tried to persuade him to see a doctor.
_____

**10** My mom ordered my little brother to stop.
_____

**11** Heavy rain in Seoul caused a river to flood.
_____

**12** The officer instructed us not to drop litter.
_____

**13** Tina has convinced me to vote for her.
_____

**14** We felt these donations to be helpful.
_____

**15** I got my dog not to bark at my neighbors.
_____

MP3

| | 3인칭/현재 | 과거 | 과거분사 |
|---|---|---|---|

**accept**

1  ~을 ~으로 받아들이다

We couldn't **accept** him **as** our leader.
우리는 그를 우리의 리더로 받아들일 수 없었다.

**believe**

2  ~가 ~라고 생각하다

He **believed** the doctor skillful.
그는 그 의사가 능숙하다고 생각했다.

**count**

3  ~을 ~라고 여기다

I **count** myself **as** an independent person.
나는 나 자신을 독립적인 사람이라고 여긴다.

**define**

4  ~을 ~라고 정의하다

Her behavior **defined** her **as** a troublemaker.
그녀의 행동이 그녀를 말썽쟁이라고 정의했다.

**describe**

5  ~을 ~라고 말하다

Marcy **describes** herself **as** a fashion designer.
마씨는 자신을 패션디자이너라고 말한다.

**imagine**

6  ~이 ~라고 상상하다

I **imagined** myself thin.
나는 나 자신이 날씬하다고 상상했다.

**know**

7  ~을 ~으로 알다

knows    knew    known

He **knows** me **as** the best teacher.
그는 나를 최고의 선생님으로 알고 있다.

## look upon
**8** ~을 ~라고 간주하다, 고려하다

I **looked upon** the dog **as** a fool.
나는 그 개를 바보라고 간주했다.

## prove
**9** ~가 ~임을 증명하다

I tried to **prove** him innocent.
나는 그가 결백하다는 것을 증명하려고 했다.

## qualify
**10** ~을 ~라고 평하다

Ms. Han **qualifies** her **as** a good person.
한 선생님은 그녀를 좋은 사람이라고 평한다.

## recognize
**11** ~을 ~으로 인정하다

We should **recognize** alcoholism **as** a disease.
우리는 알코올 중독을 병으로 인정해야 한다.

## refer to
**12** ~을 ~라고 언급하다

They **referred to** Naomi **as** a good daughter.
그들은 나오미를 좋은 딸이라고 언급했다.

## regard
**13** ~을 ~으로 여기다, 생각하다

We **regard** him **as** a friend of ours.
우리는 그를 우리의 친구라 여긴다.

## see
**14** ~을 ~으로 보다

| sees | saw | seen |

My friends **see** me **as** a genius.
내 친구들은 나를 천재로 본다.

## suppose
**15** ~가 ~일 거라 추측하다

They **supposed** Tom guilty.
그들은 탐이 유죄일 거라 추측했다.

**A** 빈칸에 알맞은 단어를 〈보기〉에서 찾아 쓰세요.

**1** We couldn't _____ him as our leader.

우리는 그를 우리의 리더로 받아들일 수 없었다.

**2** He _____ the doctor skillful.

그는 그 의사가 능숙하다고 생각했다.

**3** I _____ myself as an independent person.

나는 나 자신을 독립적인 사람이라고 여긴다.

**4** Her behavior _____ her as a troublemaker.

그녀의 행동이 그녀가 말썽쟁이라고 정의했다.

**5** Marcy _____ herself as a fashion designer.

마씨는 자신이 패션디자이너라고 말한다.

**6** I _____ myself thin.

나는 나 자신이 날씬하다고 상상했다.

**7** He _____ me as the best teacher.

그는 나를 최고의 선생님으로 알고 있다.

**8** I _____ the dog as a fool.

나는 그 개를 바보라고 간주했다.

보기
defined
accept
count
believed
describes
looked upon
knows
imagined

**B** 단어를 알맞게 배열하여 문장을 완성하세요.

**1** him | I tried to | prove | innocent.

**2** her | as a good person. | Ms. Han | qualifies

**3** We | alcoholism | should recognize | as a disease.

**4** Naomi | They | referred to | as a good daughter.

**5** him | We | regard | as a friend of ours.

**6** me | as a genius. | My friends | see

**7** They | guilty. | supposed | Tom

C 다음 문장에서 동사를 찾아 동그라미하고, 해석을 써 보세요.

1 My friends see me as a genius.
_____

2 They supposed Tom guilty.
_____

3 I count myself as an independent person.
_____

4 We regard him as a friend of ours.
_____

5 He believed the doctor skillful.
_____

6 I tried to prove him innocent.
_____

7 We should recognize alcoholism as a disease.
_____

8 I looked upon the dog as a fool.
_____

9 Marcy describes herself as a fashion designer.
_____

10 Ms. Han qualifies her as a good person.
_____

11 He knows me as the best teacher.
_____

12 They referred to Naomi as a good daughter.
_____

13 Her behavior defined her as a troublemaker.
_____

14 I imagined myself thin.
_____

15 We couldn't accept him as our leader.
_____

MP3

| | 3인칭/현재 | 과거 | 과거분사 |
|---|---|---|---|

**ask**

1 ~가 ~하기를 요청하다

I **asked** him **to** complete the story.
나는 그가 이야기를 끝내길 요청했다.

**bid**

2 ~에게 ~을 명령하다

bids   bade/bid   bidden/bid

My father **bade** me come closer.
아빠가 나에게 더 가까이 오라고 명령했다.

**beg**

3 ~에게 ~을 간청하다

She **begged** me **for** a donation.
그녀는 나에게 기부해 달라고 간청했다.

**have**

4 ~에게 ~하도록 시키다

has   had   had

He **had** Jane do her homework.
그는 제인에게 숙제하라고 시켰다.

**help**

5 ~가 ~하는 것을 돕다

Please **help** me lift this box.
제가 이 상자를 들게 도와주세요.

## ■ let
**6** ~가 ~하도록 허락하다

lets     let     let

My dad won't **let** me go on the field trip.
우리 아빠는 내가 견학 가는 것을 허락하지 않을 것이다.


## ■ make
**7** ~가 ~하게 만들다

makes     made     made

My mom always **makes** me study the whole day.
우리 엄마는 항상 내가 하루 종일 공부하게 만든다.


## ☐ paint
**8** ~을 ~로 칠하다

He **painted** the fence white.
그는 울타리를 흰색으로 칠했다.


## ☐ thank
**9** ~에게 ~에 대해 감사하다

I **thanked** him **for** his help.
나는 그의 도움에 감사했다.


## ☐ watch
**10** ~이 ~하는 것을 지켜 보다

I **watched** a duck and her ducklings cross the street.
나는 오리와 새끼오리들이 길을 건너는 것을 지켜봤다.

**A** 빈칸에 알맞은 단어를 〈보기〉에서 찾아 쓰세요.

**1** I _____ him to complete the story.

나는 그가 이야기를 끝내길 요청했다.

**2** My father _____ me come closer.

아빠는 나에게 가까이 오라고 명령했다.

**3** She _____ me for a donation.

그녀는 나에게 기부해 달라고 간청했다.

**4** He _____ Jane do her homework.

그는 제인에게 숙제하라고 시켰다.

보기
begged
asked
help
bade
had

**5** Please _____ me lift this box.

제가 이 상자를 들게 도와주세요.

**B** 단어를 알맞게 배열하여 문장을 완성하세요.

**1**　　My dad　　　　　go on the field trip.　　　　won't let　　　　me

_____

**2**　　me　　　My mom　　　always makes　　　study the whole day.

_____

**3**　　the fence　　　painted　　　white.　　　He

_____

**4**　　him　　　　I　　　　thanked　　　for his help.

_____

**5**　　I　　　cross the street.　　　watched　　　a duck and her ducklings

_____

C 두 문장의 뜻이 같도록 빈칸을 채우고, 해석을 써 보세요

**1** I thanked him for his help.

_____

**2** My dad won't let me go on the field trip.

_____

**3** I asked him to complete the story.

_____

**4** She begged me for a donation.

_____

**5** Please help me lift this box.

_____

**6** My mom always makes me study the whole day.

_____

**7** He had Jane do her homework.

_____

**8** My father bade me come closer.

_____

**9** I watched a duck and her ducklings cross the street.

_____

**10** He painted the fence white.

_____

# 동사 변화표

## Pattern 1

| | 원형 | 3인칭/현재 | 과거 | 과거분사 |
|---|---|---|---|---|
| **Day 1** | act | acts | acted | acted |
| | bark | barks | barked | barked |
| | bend | bends | bent | bent |
| | blink | blinks | blinked | blinked |
| | cough | coughs | coughed | coughed |
| | cry | cries | cried | cried |
| | dance | dances | danced | danced |
| | dig | digs | dug | dug |
| | fall | falls | fell | fallen |
| | hold | holds | held | held |
| | laugh | laughs | laughed | laughed |
| | press | presses | pressed | pressed |
| | tell | tells | told | told |
| | sing | sings | sang | sung |
| | stand | stands | stood | stood |
| **Day 2** | appear | appears | appeared | appeared |
| | arrive | arrives | arrived | arrived |
| | begin | begins | began | begun |
| | bow | bows | bowed | bowed |
| | change | changes | changed | changed |
| | climb | climbs | climbed | climbed |
| | come | comes | came | come |
| | disappear | disappears | disappeared | disappeared |
| | exist | exists | existed | existed |
| | fill | fills | filled | filled |

| | | | |
|---|---|---|---|
| finish | finishes | finished | finished |
| glance | glances | glanced | glanced |
| go | goes | went | gone |
| occur | occurs | occurred | occurred |
| stop | stops | stopped | stopped |
| **Day 3** bake | bakes | baked | baked |
| burn | burns | burned / burnt | burned / burnt |
| burst | bursts | burst | burst |
| cook | cooks | cooked | cooked |
| eat | eats | ate | eaten |
| fit | fits | fitted / fit | fitted / fit |
| float | floats | floated | floated |
| fry | fries | fried | fried |
| leak | leaks | leaked | leaked |
| open | opens | opened | opened |
| pack | packs | packed | packed |
| peel | peels | peeled | peeled |
| pile | piles | piled | piled |
| prepare | prepares | prepared | prepared |
| take care of | takes care of | took care of | taken care of |
| **Day 4** blow | blows | blew | blown |
| blossom | blossoms | blossomed | blossomed |
| cooperate | cooperates | cooperated | cooperated |
| die | dies | died | died |
| diminish | diminishes | diminished | diminished |
| escape | escapes | escaped | escaped |
| exercise | exercises | exercised | exercised |
| gather | gathers | gathered | gathered |
| glow | glows | glowed | glowed |
| hunt | hunts | hunted | hunted |

| | | | |
|---|---|---|---|
| invest | invests | invested | invested |
| jog | jogs | jogged | jogged |
| leave | leaves | left | left |
| lie | lies | lied | lied |
| meet | meets | met | met |
| **Day 5** argue | argues | argued | argued |
| balance | balances | balanced | balanced |
| behave | behaves | behaved | behaved |
| bounce | bounces | bounced | bounced |
| breathe | breathes | breathed | breathed |
| cease | ceases | ceased | ceased |
| crash | crashes | crashed | crashed |
| depart | departs | departed | departed |
| drive | drives | drove | driven |
| fly | flies | flew | flown |
| last | lasts | lasted | lasted |
| lie | lies | lay | lain |
| run | runs | ran | run |
| ski | skis | skied | skied |
| swim | swims | swam | swum |
| **Day 6** agree (with) | agrees (with) | agreed (with) | agreed (with) |
| agree (on/to) | agrees (on/to) | agreed (on/to) | agreed (on/to) |
| crack | cracks | cracked | cracked |
| disagree | disagrees | disagreed | disagreed |
| do | does | did | done |
| forget | forgets | forgot | forgotten |
| form | forms | formed | formed |
| grow | grows | grew | grown |
| help | helps | helped | helped |
| decrease | decreases | decreased | decreased |

| | | | |
|---|---|---|---|
| increase | increases | increased | increased |
| join | joins | joined | joined |
| manage | manages | managed | managed |
| move | moves | moved | moved |
| listen | listens | listened | listened |

**Day 7**

| | | | |
|---|---|---|---|
| apologize | apologizes | apologized | apologized |
| assist | assists | assisted | assisted |
| bump | bumps | bumped | bumped |
| call | calls | called | called |
| care | cares | cared | cared |
| consult | consults | consulted | consulted |
| expand | expands | expanded | expanded |
| flow | flows | flowed | flowed |
| frown | frowns | frowned | frowned |
| hurt | hurts | hurt | hurt |
| lift | lifts | lifted | lifted |
| offend | offends | offended | offended |
| slide | slides | slid | slid |
| struggle | struggles | struggled | struggled |
| yell | yells | yelled | yelled |

**Day 8**

| | | | |
|---|---|---|---|
| belong | belongs | belonged | belonged |
| consist | consists | consisted | consisted |
| drop | drops | dropped | dropped |
| figure | figures | figured | figured |
| glare | glares | glared | glared |
| happen | happens | happened | happened |
| joke | jokes | joked | joked |
| perform | performs | performed | performed |
| play | plays | played | played |
| reflect | reflects | reflected | reflected |

| | draw | draws | drew | drawn |
|---|---|---|---|---|
| | save | saves | saved | saved |
| | search | searches | searched | searched |
| | sigh | sighs | sighed | sighed |
| | think | thinks | thought | thought |
| **Day 9** | contrast | contrasts | contrasted | contrasted |
| | count | counts | counted | counted |
| | dip | dips | dipped | dipped |
| | extend | extends | extended | extended |
| | fade | fades | faded | faded |
| | follow | follows | followed | followed |
| | heat | heats | heated | heated |
| | judge | judges | judged | judged |
| | react | reacts | reacted | reacted |
| | slip | slips | slipped | slipped |
| | stick | sticks | sticked / stuck | sticked / stuck |
| | survive | survives | survived | survived |
| | tear | tears | tore | torn |
| | watch | watches | watched | watched |
| | worry | worries | worried | worried |
| **Day 10** | approve | approves | approved | approved |
| | differ | differs | differed | differed |
| | inquire | inquires | inquired | inquired |
| | learn | learns | learned / learnt | learned / learnt |
| | lock | locks | locked | locked |
| | melt | melts | melted | melted |
| | mind | minds | minded | minded |
| | participate | participates | participated | participated |
| | pick | picks | picked | picked |
| | quit | quits | quitted / quit | quitted / quit |

| | | | |
|---|---|---|---|
| read | reads | read [red] | read [red] |
| repeat | repeats | repeated | repeated |
| ride | rides | rode | ridden |
| shower | showers | showered | showered |
| swing | swings | swung | swung |
| **Day 11** aspire | aspires | aspired | aspired |
| count | counts | counted | counted |
| dream | dreams | dreamed / dreamt | dreamed / dreamt |
| dwell | dwells | dwelled | dwelled |
| emerge | emerges | emerged | emerged |
| guess | guesses | guessed | guessed |
| hear | hears | heard | heard |
| hesitate | hesitates | hesitated | hesitated |
| improve | improves | improved | improved |
| progress | progresses | progressed | progressed |
| reply | replies | replied | replied |
| sail | sails | sailed | sailed |
| see | sees | saw | seen |
| smile | smiles | smiled | smiled |
| vanish | vanishes | vanished | vanished |
| **Day 12** bet | bets | bet | bet |
| charge | charges | charged | charged |
| contribute | contributes | contributed | contributed |
| deal | deals | dealt | dealt |
| evolve | evolves | evolved | evolved |
| gamble | gambles | gambled | gambled |
| lose | loses | lost | lost |
| pause | pauses | paused | paused |
| pay | pays | paid | paid |
| qualify | qualifies | qualified | qualified |

| | | | |
|---|---|---|---|
| recover | recovers | recovered | recovered |
| settle | settles | settled | settled |
| shut | shuts | shut | shut |
| sign | signs | signed | signed |
| win | wins | won | won |
| **Day 13** insist | insists | insisted | insisted |
| matter | matters | mattered | mattered |
| resist | resists | resisted | resisted |
| respond | responds | responded | responded |
| retire | retires | retired | retired |
| return | returns | returned | returned |
| start | starts | started | started |
| subscribe | subscribes | subscribed | subscribed |
| sympathize | sympathizes | sympathized | sympathized |
| tend | tends | tended | tended |
| transfer | transfers | transferred | transferred |
| try | tries | tried | tried |
| turn | turns | turned | turned |
| vote | votes | voted | voted |
| wake | wakes | woke | woken |
| **Day 14** account | accounts | accounted | accounted |
| hang | hangs | hung | hung |
| interpret | interprets | interpreted | interpreted |
| look (at) | looks | looked | looked |
| look (for) | looks | looked | looked |
| observe | observes | observed | observed |
| operate | operates | operated | operated |
| pour | pours | poured | poured |
| rain | rains | rained | rained |
| rise | rises | rose | risen |

| | | | |
|---|---|---|---|
| | set | set | set | set |
| | sink | sinks | sank | sunken |
| | snow | snows | snowed | snowed |
| | study | studies | studied | studied |
| | vary | varies | varied | varied |
| **Day 15** | rank | ranks | ranked | ranked |
| | reach | reaches | reached | reached |
| | refer | refers | referred | referred |
| | rest | rests | rested | rested |
| | result | results | resulted | resulted |
| | rush | rushes | rushed | rushed |
| | shake | shakes | shook | shaken |
| | shout | shouts | shouted | shouted |
| | sit | sits | sat | sat |
| | sleep | sleeps | slept | slept |
| | succeed | succeeds | succeeded | succeeded |
| | suffer | suffers | suffered | suffered |
| | understand | understands | understood | understood |
| | wait | waits | waited | waited |
| | work | works | worked | worked |
| **Day 16** | chat | chats | chatted | chatted |
| | depend | depends | depend | depended |
| | dive | dives | dived / dove | dived |
| | explode | explodes | exploded | exploded |
| | gain | gains | gained | gained |
| | lead | leads | led | led |
| | proceed | proceeds | proceeded | proceeded |
| | rely | relies | relied | relied |
| | speak | speaks | spoke | spoken |
| | stay | stays | stayed | stayed |

| | | | |
|---|---|---|---|
| take place | takes place | took place | taken place |
| talk | talks | talked | talked |
| touch | touches | touched | touched |
| travel | travels | travelled | travelled |
| work | works | worked | worked |

## Pattern 2

| | | | | |
|---|---|---|---|---|
| **Day 17** | be | is | was | been |
| | be | are | were | been |
| | become | becomes | became | become |
| | come | comes | came | come |
| | fall | falls | fell | fallen |
| | get | gets | got | got / gotten |
| | go | goes | went | gone |
| | hold | holds | held | held |
| | keep | keeps | kept | kept |
| | lie | lies | lay | lain |
| | remain | remains | remained | remained |
| | run | runs | ran | run |
| | stand | stands | stood | stood |
| | stay | stays | stayed | stayed |
| **Day 18** | act | acts | acted | acted |
| | appear | appears | appeared | appeared |
| | feel | feels | felt | felt |
| | grow | grows | grew | grown |
| | look | looks | looked | looked |
| | measure | measures | measured | measured |
| | prove | proves | proved | proven |
| | seem | seems | seemed | seemed |
| | smell | smells | smelled | smelled |

|  | sound | sounds | sounded | sounded |
|  | taste | tastes | tasted | tasted |
|  | turn | turns | turned | turned |
|  | turn out | turns out | turned out | turned out |

## Pattern 3

| | | | | |
|---|---|---|---|---|
| **Day 19** | approach | approaches | approached | approached |
| | astonish | astonishes | astonished | astonished |
| | confess | confesses | confessed | confessed |
| | defend | defends | defended | defended |
| | explain | explains | explained | explained |
| | finish | finishes | finished | finished |
| | judge | judges | judged | judged |
| | keep | keeps | kept | kept |
| | learn | learns | learned / learnt | learned / learnt |
| | open | opens | opened | opened |
| | pause | pauses | paused | paused |
| | pay | pays | paid | paid |
| | perform | performs | performed | performed |
| | serve | serves | served | served |
| | wrap | wraps | wrapped | wrapped |
| **Day 20** | answer | answers | answered | answered |
| | bake | bakes | baked | baked |
| | chase | chases | chased | chased |
| | defeat | defeats | defeated | defeated |
| | enroll | enrolls | enrolled | enrolled |
| | expect | expects | expected | expected |
| | fit | fits | fitted | fitted |
| | join | joins | joined | joined |
| | lift | lifts | lifted | lifted |

| | | | |
|---|---|---|---|
| order | orders | ordered | ordered |
| owe | owes | owed | owed |
| pack | packs | packed | packed |
| plan | plans | planned | planned |
| send | sends | sent | sent |
| wipe | wipes | wiped | wiped |
| **Day 21** allow | allows | allowed | allowed |
| blink | blinks | blinked | blinked |
| capture | captures | captured | captured |
| charm | charms | charmed | charmed |
| decrease | decreases | decreased | decreased |
| determine | determines | determined | determined |
| expand | expands | expanded | expanded |
| load | loads | loaded | loaded |
| lose | loses | lost | lost |
| oppose | opposes | opposed | opposed |
| organize | organizes | organized | organized |
| play | plays | played | played |
| sell | sells | sold | sold |
| wash | washes | washed | washed |
| write | writes | wrote | written |
| **Day 22** ask | asks | asked | asked |
| bribe | bribes | bribed | bribed |
| buy | buys | bought | bought |
| celebrate | celebrates | celebrated | celebrated |
| decline | declines | declined | declined |
| introduce | introduces | introduced | introduced |
| lack | lacks | lacked | lacked |
| manage | manages | managed | managed |
| obey | obeys | obeyed | obeyed |

| | | | |
|---|---|---|---|
| offend | offends | offended | offended |
| post | posts | posted | posted |
| select | selects | selected | selected |
| test | tests | tested | tested |
| trick | tricks | tricked | tricked |
| worry | worries | worried | worried |
| **Day 23** attempt | attempts | attempted | attempted |
| build | builds | built | built |
| cease | ceases | ceased | ceased |
| chew | chews | chewed | chewed |
| decide | decides | decided | decided |
| exercise | exercises | exercised | exercised |
| interpret | interprets | interpreted | interpreted |
| lock | locks | locked | locked |
| mark | marks | marked | marked |
| melt | melts | melted | melted |
| put | puts | put | put |
| seek | seeks | sought | sought |
| toss | tosses | tossed | tossed |
| win | wins | won | won |
| wish | wishes | wished | wished |
| **Day 24** become | becomes | became | become |
| carve | carves | carved | carved |
| congratulate | congratulates | congratulated | congratulated |
| debate | debates | debated | debated |
| define | defines | defined | defined |
| exclude | excludes | excluded | excluded |
| inform | informs | informed | informed |
| leak | leaks | leaked | leaked |
| lean | leans | leaned / leant | leaned / leant |

| | | | |
|---|---|---|---|
| marry | marries | married | married |
| mount | mounts | mounted | mounted |
| search | searches | searched | searched |
| suggest | suggests | suggested | suggested |
| tear | tears | tore | torn |
| wear | wears | wore | worn |

**Day 25**

| | | | |
|---|---|---|---|
| believe | believes | believed | believed |
| board | boards | boarded | boarded |
| cancel | cancels | canceled | canceled |
| convict | convicts | convicted | convicted |
| damage | damages | damaged | damaged |
| exchange | exchanges | exchanged | exchanged |
| indicate | indicates | indicated | indicated |
| invent | invents | invented | invented |
| invest | invests | invested | invested |
| mention | mentions | mentioned | mentioned |
| read | reads | read [red] | read [red] |
| save | saves | saved | saved |
| swing | swings | swung | swung |
| watch | watches | watched | watched |
| work | worked | worked | worked |

**Day 26**

| | | | |
|---|---|---|---|
| blow | blows | blew | blown |
| book | books | booked | booked |
| calculate | calculates | calculated | calculated |
| detach | detaches | detached | detached |
| examine | examines | examined | examined |
| improve | improves | improved | improved |
| interrupt | interrupts | interrupted | interrupted |
| invade | invades | invaded | invaded |
| miss | misses | missed | missed |

| | | | |
|---|---|---|---|
| respect | respects | respected | respected |
| reveal | reveals | revealed | revealed |
| swim | swims | swam | swum |
| use | uses | used | used |
| want | wants | wanted | wanted |
| waste | wastes | wasted | wasted |

**Day 27**

| | | | |
|---|---|---|---|
| block | blocks | blocked | blocked |
| bring | brings | brought | brought |
| bury | buries | buried | buried |
| cure | cures | cured | cured |
| disappoint | disappoints | disappointed | disappointed |
| evaluate | evaluates | evaluated | evaluated |
| import | imports | imported | imported |
| insult | insults | insulted | insulted |
| intend | intends | intended | intended |
| mistake | mistakes | mistook | mistaken |
| rest | rests | rested | rested |
| steal | steals | stole | stolen |
| turn | turns | turned | turned |
| understand | understands | understood | understood |
| wake | wakes | woke | woken |

**Day 28**

| | | | |
|---|---|---|---|
| blame | blames | blamed | blamed |
| burn | burns | burned / burnt | burned / burnt |
| call | calls | called | called |
| crowd | crowds | crowded | crowded |
| distinguish | distinguishes | distinguished | distinguished |
| donate | donates | donated | donated |
| estimate | estimates | estimated | estimated |
| imagine | imagines | imagined | imagined |
| inspire | inspires | inspired | inspired |

| | | | |
|---|---|---|---|
| install | installs | installed | installed |
| observe | observes | observed | observed |
| restore | restores | restored | restored |
| return | returns | returned | returned |
| slide | slides | slid | slid |
| wait | waits | waited | waited |
| **Day 29** begin | begins | began | begun |
| bully | bullies | bullied | bullied |
| care | cares | cared | cared |
| change | changes | changed | changed |
| cover | covers | covered | covered |
| embarrass | embarrasses | embarrassed | embarrassed |
| illustrate | illustrates | illustrated | illustrated |
| inhabit | inhabits | inhabited | inhabited |
| inject | injects | injected | injected |
| obtain | obtains | obtained | obtained |
| resist | resists | resisted | resisted |
| ruin | ruins | ruined | ruined |
| slice | slices | sliced | sliced |
| try | tries | tried | tried |
| visit | visits | visited | visited |
| **Day 30** attribute | attributes | attributed | attributed |
| beat | beats | beat | beaten |
| brush | brushes | brushed | brushed |
| consider | considers | considered | considered |
| count | counts | counted | counted |
| enhance | enhances | enhanced | enhanced |
| fascinate | fascinates | fascinated | fascinated |
| imitate | imitates | imitated | imitated |
| impress | impresses | impressed | impressed |

| | | | |
|---|---|---|---|
| occupy | occupies | occupied | occupied |
| reserve | reserves | reserved | reserved |
| run | runs | ran | run |
| settle | settles | settled | settled |
| sink | sinks | sank | sunk |
| trust | trusts | trusted | trusted |

**Day 31**

| | | | |
|---|---|---|---|
| bear | bears | bore | borne |
| breathe | breathes | breathed | breathed |
| contact | contacts | contacted | contacted |
| correct | corrects | corrected | corrected |
| engage | engages | engaged | engaged |
| fasten | fastens | fastened | fastened |
| hire | hires | hired | hired |
| hunt | hunts | hunted | hunted |
| ignore | ignores | ignored | ignored |
| operate | operates | operated | operated |
| recognize | recognizes | recognized | recognized |
| represent | represents | represented | represented |
| say | says | said | said |
| sing | sings | sang | sung |
| treat | treats | treated | treated |

**Day 32**

| | | | |
|---|---|---|---|
| attend | attends | attended | attended |
| bother | bothers | bothered | bothered |
| continue | continues | continued | continued |
| copy | copies | copied | copied |
| encourage | encourages | encouraged | encouraged |
| frustrate | frustrates | frustrated | frustrated |
| hang | hangs | hung | hung |
| heal | heals | healed | healed |
| hurt | hurts | hurt | hurt |

| | | | |
|---|---|---|---|
| overcome | overcomes | overcame | overcome |
| receive | receives | received | received |
| reply | replies | replied | replied |
| see | sees | saw | seen |
| shout | shouts | shouted | shouted |
| transform | transforms | transformed | transformed |
| **Day 33** approve | approves | approved | approved |
| borrow | borrows | borrowed | borrowed |
| control | controls | controlled | controlled |
| convey | conveys | conveyed | conveyed |
| encounter | encounters | encountered | encountered |
| explore | explores | explored | explored |
| fry | fries | fried | fried |
| greet | greets | greeted | greeted |
| grip | grips | gripped | gripped |
| hit | hits | hit | hit |
| permit | permits | permitted | permitted |
| replace | replaces | replaced | replaced |
| shoot | shoots | shot | shot |
| start | starts | started | started |
| transfer | transfers | transferred | transferred |
| **Day 34** attract | attracts | attracted | attracted |
| contribute | contributes | contributed | contributed |
| cut | cuts | cut | cut |
| crack | cracks | cracked | cracked |
| emphasize | emphasizes | emphasized | emphasized |
| forgive | forgives | forgave | forgiven |
| gamble | gambles | gambled | gambled |
| grab | grabs | grabbed | grabbed |
| hide | hides | hid | hidden |

| | | | |
|---|---|---|---|
| hug | hugs | hugged | hugged |
| pick | picks | picked | picked |
| repeat | repeats | repeated | repeated |
| shake | shakes | shook | shaken |
| sort | sorts | sorted | sorted |
| trace | traces | traced | traced |
| **Day 35** attack | attacks | attacked | attacked |
| acknowledge | acknowledges | acknowledged | acknowledged |
| bomb | bombs | bombed | bombed |
| contain | contains | contained | contained |
| demand | demands | demanded | demanded |
| drive | drives | drove | driven |
| eat | eats | ate | eaten |
| fold | folds | folded | folded |
| forbid | forbids | forbade | forbidden |
| heat | heats | heated | heated |
| injure | injures | injured | injured |
| predict | predicts | predicted | predicted |
| repair | repairs | repaired | repaired |
| scan | scans | scanned | scanned |
| tour | tours | toured | toured |
| **Day 36** appreciate | appreciates | appreciated | appreciated |
| assume | assumes | assumed | assumed |
| boil | boils | boiled | boiled |
| construct | constructs | constructed | constructed |
| cook | cooks | cooked | cooked |
| design | designs | designed | designed |
| drink | drinks | drank | drunk |
| enjoy | enjoys | enjoyed | enjoyed |
| fix | fixes | fixed | fixed |

| | | | |
|---|---|---|---|
| float | floats | floated | floated |
| hear | hears | heard | heard |
| narrate | narrates | narrated | narrated |
| prefer | prefers | preferred | preferred |
| remove | removes | removed | removed |
| touch | touches | touched | touched |
| **Day 37** abandon | abandons | abandoned | abandoned |
| address | addresses | addressed | addressed |
| bless | blesses | blessed | blessed |
| confirm | confirms | confirmed | confirmed |
| do | does | did | done |
| draw | draws | drew | drawn |
| exceed | exceeds | exceeded | exceeded |
| excuse | excuses | excused | excused |
| guide | guides | guided | guided |
| peel | peels | peeled | peeled |
| prepare | prepares | prepared | prepared |
| relate | relates | related | related |
| release | releases | released | released |
| sail | sails | sailed | sailed |
| throw | throws | threw | thrown |
| **Day 38** admit | admits | admitted | admitted |
| apply | applies | applied | applied |
| blend | blends | blended | blended |
| conduct | conducts | conducted | conducted |
| doubt | doubts | doubted | doubted |
| enter | enters | entered | entered |
| evolve | evolves | evolved | evolved |
| exaggerate | exaggerate | exaggerated | exaggerated |
| face | faces | faced | faced |

| | | | |
|---|---|---|---|
| guess | guesses | guessed | guessed |
| pollute | pollutes | polluted | polluted |
| preserve | preserves | preserved | preserved |
| reject | rejects | rejected | rejected |
| rush | rushes | rushed | rushed |
| tie | ties | tied | tied |

| | | | | |
|---|---|---|---|---|
| **Day 39** | arrest | arrests | arrested | arrested |
| | bite | bites | bit | bitten |
| | choose | chooses | chose | chosen |
| | conclude | concludes | concluded | concluded |
| | enclose | encloses | enclosed | enclosed |
| | endure | endures | endured | endured |
| | feel | feels | felt | felt |
| | grow | grows | grew | grown |
| | need | needs | needed | needed |
| | offer | offers | offered | offered |
| | press | presses | pressed | pressed |
| | refuse | refuses | refused | refused |
| | rob | robs | robbed | robbed |
| | shave | shaves | shaved | shaved |
| | teach | teaches | taught | taught |

| | | | | |
|---|---|---|---|---|
| **Day 40** | bind | binds | bound | bound |
| | divide | divides | divided | divided |
| | edit | edits | edited | edited |
| | elect | elects | elected | elected |
| | establish | establishes | established | established |
| | figure | figures | figured | figured |
| | grant | grants | granted | granted |
| | mind | minds | minded | minded |
| | move | moves | moved | moved |

| | | | |
|---|---|---|---|
| prevent | prevents | prevented | prevented |
| reform | reforms | reformed | reformed |
| ride | rides | rode | ridden |
| shame | shames | shamed | shamed |
| switch | switches | switched | switched |
| yell | yells | yelled | yelled |
| **Day 41** anticipate | anticipates | anticipated | anticipated |
| bend | bends | bent | bent |
| charge | charges | charged | charged |
| divorce | divorces | divorced | divorced |
| drag | drags | dragged | dragged |
| follow | follows | followed | followed |
| gain | gains | gained | gained |
| include | includes | included | included |
| mean | means | meant | meant |
| promote | promotes | promoted | promoted |
| reduce | reduces | reduced | reduced |
| relieve | relieves | relieved | relieved |
| remind | reminds | reminded | reminded |
| see | sees | saw | seen |
| suppose | supposes | supposed | supposed |
| **Day 42** appoint | appoints | appointed | appointed |
| ban | bans | banned | banned |
| catch | catches | caught | caught |
| discuss | discusses | discussed | discussed |
| distribute | distributes | distributed | distributed |
| disturb | disturbs | disturbed | disturbed |
| escape | escapes | escaped | escaped |
| force | forces | forced | forced |
| forget | forgets | forgot | forgotten |

| | | | |
|---|---|---|---|
| make | makes | made | made |
| prove | proves | proved | proved / proven |
| qualify | qualifies | qualified | qualified |
| quit | quits | quit / quitted | quit / quitted |
| recover | recovers | recovered | recovered |
| succeed | succeeds | succeeded | succeeded |
| **Day 43** award | awards | awarded | awarded |
| cast | casts | cast | cast |
| detect | detects | detected | detected |
| discover | discovers | discovered | discovered |
| disgust | disgusts | disgusted | disgusted |
| dismiss | dismisses | dismissed | dismissed |
| fly | flies | flew | flew |
| form | forms | formed | formed |
| love | loves | loved | loved |
| love (to / -ing) | loves | loved | loved |
| pronounce | pronounces | pronounced | pronounced |
| publish | publishes | published | published |
| purchase | purchases | purchased | purchased |
| record | records | recorded | recorded |
| strike | strikes | struck | struck |
| **Day 44** await | awaits | awaited | awaited |
| carry | carries | carried | carried |
| desire | desires | desired | desired |
| destroy | destroys | destroyed | destroyed |
| disclose | discloses | disclosed | disclosed |
| discount | discounts | discounted | discounted |
| fill | fills | filled | filled |
| get | gets | got | gotten |
| look | looks | looked | looked |

| | | | |
|---|---|---|---|
| pray | prays | prayed | prayed |
| prescribe | prescribes | prescribed | prescribed |
| push | pushes | pushed | pushed |
| recommend | recommends | recommended | recommended |
| sit | sits | sat | sat |
| stretch | stretches | stretched | stretched |

**Day 45**

| | | | |
|---|---|---|---|
| attach | attaches | attached | attached |
| confront | confronts | confronted | confronted |
| consult | consults | consulted | consulted |
| demonstrate | demonstrates | demonstrated | demonstrated |
| deserve | deserves | deserved | deserved |
| dig | digs | dug | dug |
| extend | extends | extended | extended |
| have | has | had | had |
| like | likes | liked | liked |
| like to [-ing] | likes | liked | liked |
| raise | raises | raised | raised |
| rank | ranks | ranked | ranked |
| reach | reaches | reached | reached |
| solve | solves | solved | solved |
| study | studies | studied | studied |

**Day 46**

| | | | |
|---|---|---|---|
| assure | assures | assured | assured |
| confine | confines | confined | confined |
| consume | consumes | consumed | consumed |
| decorate | decorates | decorated | decorated |
| delete | deletes | deleted | deleted |
| deliver | delivers | delivered | delivered |
| express | expresses | expressed | expressed |
| help | helps | helped | helped |
| leave | leaves | left | left |

| | | | |
|---|---|---|---|
| live | lives | lived | lived |
| realize | realizes | realized | realized |
| sign | signs | signed | signed |
| supply | supplies | supplied | supplied |
| take | takes | took | taken |
| think | thinks | thought | thought |
| **Day 47** attain | attains | attained | attained |
| connect | connects | connected | connected |
| deny | denies | denied | denied |
| describe | describes | described | described |
| diminish | diminishes | diminished | diminished |
| dip | dips | dipped | dipped |
| feed | feeds | fed | fed |
| give | gives | gave | given |
| lead | leads | led | led |
| pile | piles | piled | piled |
| pour | pours | poured | poured |
| race | races | raced | raced |
| scold | scolds | scolded | scolded |
| stop | stops | stopped | stopped |
| **Day 48** assert | asserts | asserted | asserted |
| contradict | contradicts | contradicted | contradicted |
| convince | convinces | convinced | convinced |
| cultivate | cultivates | cultivated | cultivated |
| declare | declares | declared | declared |
| delay | delays | delayed | delayed |
| export | exports | exported | exported |
| hold | holds | held | held |
| influence | influences | influenced | influenced |
| know | knows | knew | known |

| | | | |
|---|---|---|---|
| recall | recalls | recalled | recalled |
| shut | shuts | shut | shut |
| support | supports | supported | supported |
| tell | tells | told | told |

## Pattern 4

| | | | | |
|---|---|---|---|---|
| **Day 49** | award | awards | awarded | awarded |
| | give | gives | gave | given |
| | guarantee | guarantees | guaranteed | guaranteed |
| | lend | lends | lent | lent |
| | mail | mails | mailed | mailed |
| | offer | offers | offered | offered |
| | order | orders | ordered | ordered |
| | owe | owes | owed | owed |
| | pour | pours | poured | poured |
| | promise | promises | promised | promised |
| **Day 50** | bring | brings | brought | brought |
| | cook | cooks | cooked | cooked |
| | charge | charges | charged | charged |
| | do | does | did | done |
| | get | gets | got | gotten |
| | refuse | refuses | refused | refused |
| | sell | sells | sold | sold |
| | take | takes | took | taken |
| | tell | tells | told | told |
| | throw | throws | threw | thrown |
| **Day 51** | hand | hands | handed | handed |
| | loan | loans | loaned | loaned |
| | pass | passes | passed | passed |
| | pay | pays | paid | paid |

| | | | |
|---|---|---|---|
| play | plays | played | played |
| read | reads | read [red] | read [red] |
| send | sends | sent | sent |
| show | shows | showed | showed / shown |
| teach | teaches | taught | taught |
| write | writes | wrote | written |

**Day 52**

| | | | |
|---|---|---|---|
| ask | asks | asked | asked |
| buy | buys | bought | bought |
| cost | costs | cost | cost |
| inform | informs | informed | informed |
| find | finds | found | found |
| grant | grants | granted | granted |
| make | makes | made | made |
| save | saves | saved | saved |
| warn | warns | warned | warned |
| wish | wishes | wished | wished |

## Pattern 5

**Day 53**

| | | | |
|---|---|---|---|
| appoint | appoints | appointed | appointed |
| boil | boils | boiled | boiled |
| call | calls | called | called |
| catch | catches | caught | caught |
| consider | considers | considered | considered |
| declare | declares | declared | declared |
| find | finds | found | found |
| hear | hears | heard | heard |
| judge | judges | judged | judged |
| keep | keeps | kept | kept |
| leave | leaves | left | left |
| make | makes | made | made |

| | | | |
|---|---|---|---|
| name | names | named | named |
| push | pushes | pushed | pushed |
| urge | urges | urged | urged |
| **Day 54** advise | advises | advised | advised |
| allow | allows | allowed | allowed |
| desire | desires | desired | desired |
| enable | enables | enabled | enabled |
| encourage | encourages | encouraged | encouraged |
| expect | expects | expected | expected |
| forbid | forbids | forbade | forbid / forbidden |
| force | forces | forced | forced |
| lead | leads | led | led |
| promote | promotes | promoted | promoted |
| recommend | recommends | recommended | recommended |
| request | requests | requested | requested |
| require | requires | required | required |
| teach | teaches | taught | taught |
| trade | trades | traded | traded |
| **Day 55** cause | causes | caused | caused |
| convince | convinces | convinced | convinced |
| elect | elects | elected | elected |
| feel | feels | felt | felt |
| get | gets | got | gotten |
| instruct | instructs | instructed | instructed |
| order | orders | ordered | ordered |
| persuade | persuades | persuaded | persuaded |
| remind | reminds | reminded | reminded |
| tell | tells | told | told |
| think | thinks | thought | thought |
| trust | trusts | trusted | trusted |

| | | | |
|---|---|---|---|
| want | wants | wanted | wanted |
| warn | warns | warned | warned |
| wish | wishes | wished | wished |
| **Day 56** accept | accepts | accepted | accepted |
| believe | believes | believed | believed |
| count | counts | counted | counted |
| define | defines | defined | defined |
| describe | describes | described | described |
| imagine | imagines | imagined | imagined |
| know | knows | knew | known |
| look upon | looks upon | looked upon | looked upon |
| prove | proves | proved | proved |
| qualify | qualifies | qualified | qualified |
| recognize | recognizes | recognized | recognized |
| refer (to) | refers | referred | referred |
| regard | regards | regarded | regarded |
| see | sees | saw | seen |
| suppose | supposes | supposed | supposed |
| **Day 57** ask | asks | asked | asked |
| beg | begs | begged | begged |
| bid | bids | bade / bid | bidden / bid |
| have | has | had | had |
| help | helps | helped | helped |
| let | lets | let | let |
| make | makes | made | made |
| paint | paints | painted | painted |
| thank | thanks | thanked | thanked |
| watch | watches | watched | watched |

# Index